The Beauty of Mary

Compiled and edited by
Rosemary Vaccari Mysel
Andrew J. Vaccari
Peter I. Vaccari

Pauline
BOOKS & MEDIA
Boston

Library of Congress Cataloging-in-Publication Data

The beauty of Mary / compiled and edited by Rosemary Vaccari Mysel, Andrew J. Vaccari, Peter I. Vaccari.

   p. cm.

Includes bibliographical references and index.

  ISBN 0-8198-1170-X (pbk. : alk. paper) 1. Mary, Blessed Virgin, Saint. I. Mysel, Rosemary Vaccari. II. Vaccari, Andrew J. III. Vaccari, Peter I.

  BT603.B43   2008

  232.91—dc22

                              2008009316

Cover design by Rosana Usselmann

Cover art: *The Annunciation*—detail of the Virgin's face. Oil on wood. Rogier (Roger) van der Weyden (c. 1399–1464). Photo: Gerard Blot. Louvre, Paris, France. Photo credit: Réunion des Musées Nationaux / Art Resource, NY.

Published by Pauline Books & Media, 50 Saint Paul's Avenue, Boston, MA 02130-3491 www.pauline.org.

Printed in the U.S.A.

Pauline Books & Media is the publishing house of the Daughters of St. Paul, an international congregation of women religious serving the Church with the communications media.

1 2 3 4 5 6 7 8 9   12 11 10 09 08

Dedication

We dedicate this work on the Blessed Virgin Mary to our mother, Lorraine Vaccari. She has always been a strong, attentive, and loving mother who has exemplified the meaning of Mary's faith-filled "yes" to do God's will. Her devotion to the Virgin Mary has challenged and inspired us on our life's journey to love God from the depth of our hearts, to cherish and appreciate the beauty of family life, and to love and serve Christ in his body, the Catholic Church. We will be forever grateful!

Contents

PART ONE

The Marian Mission

—◦◦◦◦—

PART TWO

Marian Mediation in the Mission of the Church

———∽◦◦∽———

Preface

Within the history of the drama of salvation, God chose and invited a young Jewish woman, Mary of Nazareth, to be the mother of the Redeemer of the world. At the moment of the Annunciation (Lk 1:26–38), Mary's "yes" to accept that role was the most dramatic and significant response ever recorded in human history.

This volume traces the story of faith and love that is found in the maternal heart of Mary. Mary of Nazareth, who became the mother of God by divine design and her co-operation, continues to accompany the Church in her own pilgrimage of faith. God uniquely chose Mary for a mission. She also symbolically represents the model of the human response to God's plan for the unfolding of the divine-human drama in history, the meaning of the true disciple of the Lord. She serves as an image of the mystery of the Church during her pilgrimage on earth and also in her fulfillment at the end of time.

This text is meant as a companion for moments of prayer. In Part One, we have chosen those texts in the New Testament that identify the Virgin Mary's critical mission in our salvation. The writers selected are from the Catholic tradition and the Orthodox tradition, and their reflections on the texts will lead us to a deeper understanding of their meaning when taken into prayer. We are profoundly aware of the limitations placed on the number of selections by virtue of space and the desire to present a text that will provide adequate material for reflection. We hope that the reader's interest will foster a desire to go to the entire text, which will identify the internal references and notes that we have not included, and to go to many other authors who have contributed to the treasury of Catholic literature on the place of the Virgin Mary in the mystery of Christ and the mystery of the Church. In Part Two, we explore the unique role of Mary's mediation in the mission of the Church. Here we have followed the liturgical cycle of feasts that appear in the calendar year. While we would have liked to include further selections from the abundance of devotional prayers, litanies, and national shrines devoted to the Blessed Virgin Mary, such an attempt would have far exceeded the possibilities of this single volume. The outstanding feature of every Marian shrine, wherever it is located throughout the world, is its eucharistic heart. The Virgin Mother of God, the God-bearer (in Greek, the *Theotokos*), accompanies us on our daily journey to her Son, especially in the interior pilgrimage of the heart.

We wish to express our deep and sincere gratitude to the many people who assisted us in this project. Their enthusiasm, support, and advice have made an enormous contribution to this work. We are particularly grateful to Elyse Hayes, the director of Library Services at the Seminary of the Immaculate Conception, and her entire staff. We thank Linda Lambeth from Madonna House Publications; Sister Margaret Hansen, OCO, prioress of the Carmelite Monastery in Pewaukee, Wisconsin; Donna Westley, the archivist of the Sisters, Servants of the Immaculate Heart of Mary; Mary Elizabeth Sperry, associate director at the United States Conference of Catholic Bishops Publishing office; Michael P. Duricy, from The Marian Library/International Marian Research Institute; and Virginia Kimball for her revised version of the poem "A Moment of Nativity."

Our deep gratitude goes to our publisher, Pauline Books & Media. Sister Madonna Ratliff, FSP, offered early support and encouragement. Sister Marianne Lorraine Trouvé, FSP, and her entire staff, through their professional guidance, editorial review, patience, and prompt responses to our concerns and questions made this project a truly collaborative venture. Their commitment to the evangelization of culture through the media has been truly inspirational. Brad McCracken and Debra Lavelle have offered indispensable guidance in our efforts to contact the copyright holders of the texts included in this volume. We assume responsibility for any shortcoming.

Part One

The Marian Mission

Mary's Place in God's Plan

B ut when the fullness of time had come, God sent his Son, born of a woman, born under the law, to ransom those under the law, so that we might receive adoption. As proof that you are children, God sent the spirit of his Son into our hearts, crying out, "Abba, Father!"

GALATIANS 4:4–6

Pope John Paul II (1978–2005) wrote many texts dedicated to the significance of Mary's place in the divine plan of salvation. His encyclical letter Redemptoris Mater (Mother of the Redeemer), *published on the feast of the Annunciation, March 25, 1987, considers St. Paul's treatment of God's plan in history and the time of the mystery of the Incarnation.*

The Mother of the Redeemer has a precise place in the plan of salvation, for "when the time had fully come, God sent forth his Son, born of woman, born under the law, to redeem those who were under the law, so that we might receive adoption as sons. And because you are sons, God has sent the Spirit of his Son into our hearts, crying, 'Abba! Father!'" (Gal 4:4–6).

With these words of the Apostle Paul, which the Second Vatican Council takes up at the beginning of its treatment of the Blessed Virgin Mary, I too wish to begin my reflection on the role of Mary in the mystery of Christ and on her active and exemplary presence in the life of the Church. For they are words which celebrate together the love of the Father, the mission of the Son, the gift of the Spirit, the role of the woman from whom the Redeemer was born, and our own divine filiation, in the mystery of the "fullness of time." This "fullness" indicates the moment fixed from all eternity when the Father sent his Son "that whoever believes in him should not perish but have eternal life" (Jn 3:16). It denotes the blessed moment when the Word that "was with God ... became flesh and dwelt among us" (Jn 1:1, 14), and made himself our brother. It marks the moment when the Holy Spirit, who had already infused the fullness of grace into Mary of Nazareth, formed in her virginal womb the human nature of Christ.

This "fullness" marks the moment when, with the entrance of the eternal into time, time itself is redeemed, and being filled with the mystery of Christ becomes definitively "salvation time." Finally, this "fullness" designates the hidden beginning of the Church's journey. In the liturgy the Church salutes Mary of Nazareth as the Church's own beginning, for in the event of the Immaculate Conception the Church sees projected, and anticipated in her most noble member, the saving grace of Easter. And above all, in the Incarnation she encounters Christ and Mary indissolubly joined: he who is the Church's Lord and Head and she who, uttering the first *fiat* of the New Covenant, prefigures the Church's condition as spouse and mother.

Pope John Paul II, *Redemptoris Mater*
(Boston: Pauline Books & Media, 1987), no. 1.[*]

---

[*] Numbers following papal documents refer to the paragraph in the document cited, not the page number.

The Annunciation

In the sixth month, the angel Gabriel was sent from God to a town of Galilee called Nazareth, to a virgin betrothed to a man named Joseph, of the house of David, and the virgin's name was Mary. And coming to her, he said, "Hail, favored one! The Lord is with you." But she was greatly troubled at what was said and pondered what sort of greeting this might be. Then the angel said to her, "Do not be afraid, Mary, for you have found favor with God. Behold, you will conceive in your womb and bear a son, and you shall name him Jesus. He will be great and will be called Son of the Most High, and the Lord God will give him the throne of David his father, and he will rule over the house of Jacob forever, and of his kingdom there will be no end." But Mary said to the angel, "How can this be, since I have no relations with a man?" And the angel said to her in reply, "The holy Spirit will come upon you, and the power of the Most High will overshadow you. Therefore the child to be born will be called holy, the Son of God. And behold, Elizabeth, your relative, has also conceived a son in her old age, and this is the sixth month for her who was called barren; for nothing will be impossible for God."

Mary said, "Behold, I am the handmaid of the Lord. May it be done to me according to your word." Then the angel departed from her.

LUKE 1:26–38

St. Irenaeus (second century) was a theologian, bishop, and martyr whose feast is celebrated on June 28. In his principal work, Against the Heresies (AH), *St. Irenaeus contrasted the disobedience of Eve with the obedience of Mary. The theme of Mary as the "new Eve" became very significant in Catholic theology, spirituality, the documents of the Church, and in art. Here he writes:*

For just as the former [Eve] was led astray by the word of an angel [the devil], so that she fled from God when she had transgressed His word; so did the latter [Mary], by an angelic communication, receive the glad tidings that she should sustain … God, being obedient to His word. And if the former did disobey God, yet the latter was persuaded to be obedient to God, in order that the Virgin Mary might become the patroness … of the virgin Eve. And thus, as the human race fell into bondage to death by means of a virgin, so is it rescued by a virgin; virginal disobedience having been balanced in the opposite scale by virginal obedience.

St. Irenaeus, *Against the Heresies* V, XIX, 1–2, in *The Ante-Nicene Fathers*, ed. Rev. Alexander Roberts, DD, and James Donaldson, LLD, vol. I (New York: Charles Scribner's Sons, 1903), 547.

In this selection from his encyclical Redemptoris Mater, *Pope John Paul II reflects on Mary's vocation to be the Mother of God. The expression "full of grace" actually becomes her new name, indicating the fullness of grace she received for her unique vocation.*

Mary is definitively *introduced into the mystery of Christ through* this event: *the Annunciation* by the angel. This takes place at Nazareth, within the concrete circumstances of the history of Israel, the people which first received God's promises. The divine messenger says to the Virgin: "Hail, full of grace, the Lord is with you" (Lk 1:28). Mary "was greatly troubled at the saying, and considered in her mind what sort of greeting this might be" (Lk 1:29): what could those extraordinary words mean, and in particular the expression "full of grace" (*kecharitoméne*).

If we wish to meditate together with Mary on these words, and especially on the expression "full of grace," we can find a significant echo in the very passage from the *Letter to the Ephesians* quoted above. And if after the announcement of the heavenly messenger the Virgin of Nazareth is also called "blessed among women" (cf. Lk 1:42), it is because of that blessing with which "God the Father" has filled us "in the heavenly places, in Christ."

It is a *spiritual blessing* which is meant for all people and which bears in itself fullness and universality ("every blessing"). It flows from that love which, in the Holy Spirit, unites the consubstantial Son to the Father. At the same time, it is a blessing poured out through Jesus Christ upon human history until the end: upon all people. This blessing, however, refers *to Mary in a special and exceptional degree:* for she was greeted by Elizabeth as "blessed among women."

The double greeting is due to the fact that in the soul of this "daughter of Sion" there is manifested, in a sense, all the "glory of grace," that grace which "the Father ... has given us in his beloved Son." For the messenger greets Mary as "full of grace"; he calls her thus as if it were her real name. He does not call her by her proper earthly name: Miryam (= Mary), but *by this new name: "full of grace."* What does this name mean? Why does the archangel address the Virgin of Nazareth in this way?

In the language of the Bible "grace" means a special gift, which according to the New Testament has its source precisely in the Trinitarian life of God himself, God who is love (cf. Jn 4:8). The fruit of this love is *"the election"* of which the *Letter to the Ephesians* speaks. On the part of God, this election is the eternal desire to save man through a sharing in his own life (cf. 2 Pt 1:4) in Christ: it is salvation through a sharing in supernatural life. The effect of this eternal gift, of this grace of man's election by God, is like a *seed of holiness,* or a spring which rises in the soul as a gift from God himself, who through grace gives life and holiness to those who are chosen. In this way there is fulfilled, that is to say there comes about, that "blessing" of man "with every spiritual blessing," that "being his adopted sons and daughters ... in Christ," in him who is eternally the "beloved Son" of the Father.

When we read that the messenger addresses Mary as "full of grace," the Gospel context, which mingles revelations and ancient promises, enables us to understand that among all the "spiritual blessings in Christ" this is a special "blessing." In the mystery of Christ she is *present* even "before the creation of the world," as the one whom the Father "has chosen" *as Mother* of his Son in the Incarnation. And, what is more, together with the Father, the Son has chosen her, entrusting her eternally to the Spirit of holiness. In an entirely special and exceptional way Mary is united to Christ, and similarly she *is eternally loved in this "beloved Son,"* this Son who is of one being with the Father, in whom is concentrated all the "glory of grace." At the same time, she is and remains perfectly open to this "gift from above" (cf. Jas 1:17). As the Council teaches, Mary "stands out among the poor and humble of the Lord, who confidently await and receive salvation from him."

If the greeting and the name "full of grace" say all this, in the context of the angel's announcement they refer first of all *to the election of Mary as Mother of the Son of God.* But at the same time the "fullness of grace" indicates all the supernatural munificence from which Mary benefits by being chosen and destined to be the Mother of Christ. If this election is fundamental for the accomplishment of God's salvific designs for humanity, and if the eternal choice in Christ and the vocation to the dignity of adopted children is the destiny of everyone, then the election of Mary is wholly exceptional and unique. Hence also the singularity and uniqueness of her place in the mystery of Christ.

The divine messenger says to her: "Do not be afraid, Mary, for you have found favor with God. And behold, you will conceive in your womb and bear a son, and you shall call his name Jesus. He will be great, and will be called the Son of the Most High" (Lk 1:30–32). And when the Virgin, disturbed by that extraordinary greeting, asks: "How shall this be, since I have no husband?" she receives from the angel the confirmation and explanation of the preceding words. Gabriel says to her: "*The Holy Spirit will come upon you*, and the power of the Most High will overshadow you; therefore the child to be born will be called holy, the Son of God" (Lk 1:35).

The Annunciation, therefore, is the revelation of the mystery of the Incarnation at the very beginning of its fulfillment on earth. God's salvific giving of himself and his life, in some way to all creation but directly to man, reaches *one of its high points in the mystery of the Incarnation.* This is indeed a high point among all the gifts of grace conferred in the history of man and of the universe: Mary is "full of grace," because it is precisely in her that the Incarnation of the Word, the hypostatic union of the Son of God with human nature, is accomplished and fulfilled. As the Council says, Mary is "the Mother of the Son of God. As a result she is also the favorite daughter of the Father and the temple of the Holy Spirit. Because of this gift of sublime grace, she far surpasses all other creatures, both in heaven and on earth."

Pope John Paul II, *Redemptoris Mater*, nos. 8 and 9.

Caryll Houselander (1901–1954) was an English Catholic laywoman, artist, and popular spiritual writer in the 1940s and 1950s. Maisie

*Ward, a leading author and publisher for twentieth-century Catholic
apologetics, wrote a biography of Houselander in which she dubbed her
the "divine eccentric" due to her solitary personality and the depth of her
spiritual insight. Houselander's corpus of writing connects the mystery of
the Incarnation and the paschal mystery of Jesus to those suffering from
the ravages of war, poverty, and the empty but seductive temptations of
a false philosophical worldview. In Houselander's work* The Reed of
God *(1944) she considers the meaning of the Annunciation.*

The church keeps the Feast of the Annunciation on the
twenty-fifth of March. There is still a touch of austerity upon
the earth, there is still a silver emptiness in the skies, but
expectation of spring is already stirring the human heart, the
bud is beginning to break on the tree, the promise of blossom
has quickened the spirit of man.

This is the season when we celebrate the wedding of the
Holy Spirit with humanity, the wedding of the Spirit of
Wisdom and Love with the dust of the earth.

I think the most moving fact in the whole history of
mankind is that wherever the Holy Spirit has desired to
renew the face of the earth He has chosen to do so through
communion with some humble little human creature.

In the instances we know of, it has not been to great or
powerful people that the Spirit has come but to the little or
the frightened, and we have seen them made new, and
known that the subsequent flowering of their lives was nothing else but Christ given to them by that sweet impact.

It is always a love story, a culmination of love between the
Spirit of Light and the Bride of the Spirit.

This is something which can happen to everyone now,
but it could not have happened to anyone but for the *fiat* of

the peasant girl in Nazareth whom the whole world calls Our Lady.

It is in Our Lady that God fell in love with Humanity.

It is upon her that the Dove descended, and the love of God for Humanity culminated in the conception of Christ in the human race.

When she surrendered herself to God, there was indeed a miraculous New Heaven and New Earth. The Spirit entered the world—light and wisdom and love, patience, fortitude, and joy entered the human heart and mind, and in the sight of God a springtime of loveliness woke in the world.

In the virginal emptiness of the girl, Mary of Nazareth, Christ was conceived; it was the wedding of God to a human child, and the wonder of it filled the earth for all time.

"He hath set His tabernacle in the sun: and He is as a bridegroom coming out of His bride chamber. His going out is from the end of heaven: and His circuit even to the end thereof" (Ps xviii [18], Gradual of the Mass of Ember Saturday in Advent).

Christ's insistence on the power of children is very striking.

Almost more than anything else in the Gospel it proves that in God's eyes *being* something comes before *doing* something.

He sets a little child among his apostles as an example of what He loves. He says that heaven is full of children.

Indeed, the Architect of Love has built the door into heaven so low that no one but a small child can pass through it, unless, to get down to a child's little height, he goes in on his knees.

How consistent it is with the incredible tenderness of God that His Christ, the Immortal Child, should be conceived by the power of the Spirit in the body of a child. That a child should bear a Child, to redeem the world.

Our Lady was at the most fourteen when the angel came to her; perhaps she was younger.

The whole world trembled on the word of a child, on a child's consent.

To what was she asked to consent?

First of all, to the descent of the Holy Spirit, to surrender her littleness to the Infinite Love, and as a result to become the Mother of Christ.

It was so tremendous, yet so passive.

She was not asked to do anything herself, but to let something be done to her.

She was not asked to renounce anything, but to receive an incredible gift.

She was not asked to lead a special kind of life, to retire to the temple and live as a nun, to cultivate suitable virtues or claim special privileges.

She was simply to remain in the world, to go forward with her marriage to Joseph, to live the life of an artisan's wife, just what she had planned to do when she had no idea that anything out of the ordinary would ever happen to her.

It almost seemed as if God's becoming man and being born of a woman *were* ordinary.

The whole thing was to happen secretly. There was to be no announcement.

The psalmists had hymned Christ's coming on harps of gold. The prophets had foretold it with burning tongues. But now the loudest telling of His presence on earth was to be the heartbeat within the heartbeat of a child.

It was to be a secret and God was so jealous of His secret that He even guarded it at the cost of His little bride's seeming dishonour.

He allowed Joseph to misjudge her, at least for a time.

This proved that God knew Our Lady's trust in Him was absolutely without limit. Everything that He did to her in the future emphasized the same thing. His trust in her trust in Him.

The one thing that He did ask of her was the gift of her humanity. She was to give Him her body and soul unconditionally, and what in this new light would have seemed absurdly trivial to anyone but the Child Bride of Wisdom— she was to give Him her daily life.

And outwardly it would not differ from the life she would have led if she had not been chosen to be the Bride of the Spirit and the Mother of God at all!

She was not even asked to live it alone with this God who was her own Being and whose Being was to be hers.

No, He asked for her ordinary life shared with Joseph. She was not to neglect her simple human tenderness, her love for an earthly man, because God was her unborn child.

On the contrary, the hands and feet, the heart, the waking, sleeping, and eating that were forming Christ were to form Him in service to Joseph.

Yes, it certainly seemed that God wanted to give the world the impression that it is ordinary for Him to be born of a human creature.

Well, that is a fact. God did mean it to be the ordinary

thing, for it is His will that Christ shall be born in every human being's life and not, as a rule, through extraordinary things, but through the ordinary daily life and the human love that people give to one another.

Our Lady said yes.

She said yes for us all.

It was as if the human race were a little dark house, without light or air, locked and latched.

The wind of the Spirit had beaten on the door, rattled the windows, tapped on the dark glass with the tiny hands of flowers, flung golden seed against it, even, in hours of storm, lashed it with the boughs of a great tree—the prophecy of the Cross—and yet the Spirit was outside. But one day a girl opened the door, and the little house was swept pure and sweet by the wind. Seas of light swept through it, and the light remained in it; and in that little house a Child was born and the Child was God.

Our Lady said yes for the human race. Each one of us must echo that yes for our own lives.

We are all asked if we will surrender what we are, our humanity, our flesh and blood, to the Holy Spirit and allow Christ to fill the emptiness formed by the particular shape of our life.

The surrender that is asked of us includes complete and absolute trust; it must be like Our Lady's surrender, without condition and without reservation.

We shall not be asked to do more than the Mother of God; we shall not be asked to become extraordinary or set apart or to make a hard and fast rule of life or to compile a manual of mortifications or heroic resolutions; we shall not be asked to cultivate our souls like rare hothouse flowers; we shall not, most of us, even be allowed to do that.

What we shall be asked to give is our flesh and blood, our daily life—our thoughts, our service to one another, our affections and loves, our words, our intellect, our waking, working, and sleeping, our ordinary human joys and sorrows—to God.

To surrender all that we are, as we are, to the Spirit of Love in order that our lives may bear Christ into the world— that is what we shall be asked.

Our Lady has made this possible. Her *fiat* was for herself and for us, but if we want God's will to be completed in us as it is in her, we must echo her *fiat*.

This is not quite such an easy thing to do as it seems.

Most people, unless the invitation comes to them in early childhood, have already thrust down fierce roots into the heavy clay of the world. Their hands are already gripping hard on to self-interest. They are already partly paralysed by fear.

To put aside suddenly every motive except this single one, the forming of Christ in our life, is not so easy for ordinary people who are to remain ordinary.

Caryll Houselander, *The Reed of God* (Westminster, MD: Christian Classics, 1987), 9–14.

The Visitation

During those days Mary set out and traveled to the hill country in haste to a town of Judah, where she entered the house of Zechariah and greeted Elizabeth. When Elizabeth heard Mary's greeting, the infant leaped in her womb, and Elizabeth, filled with the holy Spirit, cried out in a loud voice and said, "Most blessed are you among women, and blessed is the fruit of your womb. And how does this happen to me, that the mother of my Lord should come to me? For at the moment the sound of your greeting reached my ears, the infant in my womb leaped for joy. Blessed are you who believed that what was spoken to you by the Lord would be fulfilled."

LUKE 1:39–45

Maisie Ward (1889–1975) was born in England, where she was raised in a well-known Catholic family. In 1916, she was instrumental in establishing the Catholic Evidence Guild. Through the Guild, she met the Australian lawyer, Francis J. Sheed, whom she married in April 1926. They cofounded the publishing house of Sheed and Ward. Together with Frank Sheed, Maisie Ward was a leading author, lecturer, and

publisher for twentieth-century Catholic apologetics. She also devoted much of her energy to the integral link that she saw between Catholic theology and spirituality and its application in the area of social justice. In the meditation below, taken from her work The Splendor of the Rosary *(1945), a book that includes prayers composed by Caryll Houselander (whose biography was written by Ward), and art from the Renaissance painter Fra Angelico, Ward offers a meditation on the second Joyful Mystery of the Rosary.*

Our Lord in this Mystery has not only taken a human nature from Mary but has left Himself helpless, powerless in the darkness of her womb to be taken where she wills. It is the beginning of a divine economy of grace whereby God saves mankind by giving Himself into the power of men.

The Cure d'Ars, marvelling over the Blessed Sacrament, said: "I bear Him to the right and He stays to the right; I bear Him to the left, and He stays to the left."

Alone of all creatures Mary was utterly worthy of her trust. Henceforward, wherever she went she would bring Jesus. It is noteworthy how in the Church when any special devotion to Our Lady is started it develops into devotion to the Blessed Sacrament—at Lourdes, for instance. Pilgrims came at first for the grotto and were chiefly healed there. But later the great moment became that of the procession of the Blessed Sacrament—the Gospel invocations "Lord, if Thou wilt Thou canst make me whole!" "Lord that I may see: Lord that I May hear!" And now cures follow the lowering of the monstrance onto the sick man's head. So, too, Father Thurston says that Benediction originated in the singing of *laude*, or canticles to Our Lady. Presently these were sung before the Blessed Sacrament was exposed, and finally the blessing by the priest with the Host transformed the service into Benediction.

In this Mystery Mary had brought Jesus with her. Elizabeth, too, was carrying a child—John the Baptist. The Gospel tells us that John leaped in his mother's womb and Elizabeth was filled with the Holy Ghost: the Church tells us that at that instant he received supernatural life, in fulfillment of what the angel had foretold to Zachary, his father: "And he shall be filled with the Holy Ghost even from his mother's womb."

Our Lady was conceived, John was born, with sanctifying grace in the soul and thus freed from the worst effect of Adam's fall—for they were so close to the Redeemer whose death was to bring new life to all mankind.

These few verses of the Gospels contain material for endless meditation. We shall never exhaust Mary's *Magnificat*, which contains the clue to all our social problems and the key to true human living. To begin by "magnifying" God and rejoicing in Him is the path to recognizing our own nothingness. Because Our Lady was utterly humble all generations would call her blessed. Only to the humble can God safely entrust his gifts: "He hath put down the mighty from their seat and hath exalted the humble." Later on, in the Sermon on the Mount, Our Lord would bless hunger and thirst after justice. Already Our Lady knows that to be filled we must first hunger. "He hath filled the hungry with good things: the rich he hath sent empty away." Surely every one should learn the *Magnificat* by heart.

Saying the Rosary, we usually think only of the moment of meeting between Our Lady and St. Elizabeth. But the

Visitation was a long visit: it lasted three months. Let us picture what two women expecting their babies would do together; what did we do, those of us who had babies? Make their tiny clothes: think about them. Then there would be the housework. Elizabeth was old and must have welcomed Mary's help: she probably got tired, and Mary made her rest. We shall each have our own imaginations about this, and they all help to make the Mystery vivid. I like to think of Our Lady filling the house with flowers to please herself and her cousin. But the background of it all was the baby near their hearts. When we are going to have a baby we are apt to think he may be a great man, to pray about his future, sometimes to be afraid about it. Elizabeth knew her baby was to be the prophet of God: Mary knew her baby was God: both of them had studied the prophecies. What trust in God Our Lady must have had to go forward unafraid.

Maisie Ward, *The Splendor of the Rosary*
(New York: Sheed and Ward, 1945), 68–70.

Most Reverend Antonio Bello (1935–1993) was ordained a priest in 1957. After serving on a seminary faculty and as a pastor, he was ordained a bishop in 1982. He served as Italian national president of the Pax Christi movement. The selections below, taken from his book Mary: Human and Holy, *offer a series of reflections on Mary's period of pregnancy and expectation.*

Holy Mary, woman with child . . .

Holy Mary, woman with child, in your virginal body you offered to the Eternal God a home in time. Tender vessel wherein God enclosed himself—though the heavens cannot contain him—we will never know how you spoke to him. You felt him leaping under your heart. Perhaps in those moments you asked yourself if you gave him his heartbeat, or if he lent you his.

You kept vigil with anxious dreams. While you worked at the loom with its shuttles whirring, and prepared woolen cloths for him with speedy hands, you also slowly wove him a tunic of flesh in the silence of your womb....

Holy Mary, we thank you because, while you carried Jesus in your womb for nine months, you carry each of us all our lives. Give us your virtues. Transform our features into those of your spirit. When our heavenly birthday arrives and the gates of heaven open wide to us, it will only be because we have come to resemble you—however slight that resemblance may be.

Holy Mary, woman of acceptance ...

Holy Mary, woman of acceptance, help us to accept the Word in the intimacy of our hearts. Help us understand, as you did, how God acts in our lives. He does not knock at the door to evict us, but to fill our loneliness with light. He does not come into our house to put us in handcuffs, but to restore to us true freedom....

Holy Mary, monstrance of Jesus' body taken down from the cross, receive us when we have surrendered our spirit. Give to our death the trusting quiet of one resting his head on his mother's shoulder and falling peacefully asleep. Hold us for a while on your lap, just as you have held us in your heart all our lives. Perform over us the rituals of final purification. Carry us at last in your arms to the Eternal One. If you present us, we will surely find mercy.

Antonio Bello, *Mary: Human and Holy*, trans. Paul Duggan (Boston: Pauline Books & Media, 2000), 35–36, 39, 41.

Mary's Canticle or Magnificat[*]

And Mary said: "My soul proclaims the greatness
of the Lord;
my spirit rejoices in God my savior.
For he has looked upon his handmaid's lowliness;
behold, from now on will all ages call me blessed.
The Mighty One has done great things for me,
and holy is his name.
His mercy is from age to age
to those who fear him.
He has shown might with his arm,
dispersed the arrogant of mind and heart.
He has thrown down the rulers from their thrones
but lifted up the lowly.
The hungry he has filled with good things;
the rich he has sent away empty.
He has helped Israel his servant,
remembering his mercy,
according to his promise to our fathers,
to Abraham and to his descendants forever."

[*] The village of Ein Kerem is located in the present-day suburbs of
Jerusalem. There, in the home of Zachary and Elizabeth, Mary met her
cousin Elizabeth. A wall in the sanctuary contains ceramic plaques with the
text of the Magnificat in over seventy-five languages.

Mary remained with her about three months and then returned to her home.

LUKE 1:46–56

Pope John Paul II returns to the theme of Mary's faith in this excerpt from Redemptoris Mater. *He sees in Mary's faith the key that opens the door to our understanding of her life and mission.*

When Elizabeth greeted her young kinswoman coming from Nazareth, *Mary replied with the Magnificat.* In her greeting, Elizabeth first called Mary "blessed" because of "the fruit of her womb," and then she called her "blessed" because of her faith (cf. Lk 1:42, 45). These two blessings referred directly to the Annunciation. Now, at the Visitation, when Elizabeth's greeting bears witness to that culminating moment, Mary's faith acquires a new consciousness and a new expression. That which remained hidden in the depths of the "obedience of faith" at the Annunciation can now be said to spring forth like a clear and life-giving flame of the spirit. The words used by Mary on the threshold of Elizabeth's house are *an inspired profession of her faith*, in which *her response to the revealed word* is expressed with the religious and poetical exultation of her whole being toward God. In these sublime words, which are simultaneously very simple and wholly inspired by the sacred texts of the people of Israel, Mary's personal experience, the ecstasy of her heart, shines forth. In them shines a ray of the mystery of God, the glory of his ineffable holiness, the eternal *love which, as an irrevocable gift, enters into human history.*

Pope John Paul II, *Redemptoris Mater*, no. 36.

Sister Mary Catherine Nolan, OP (1933–), is an Adrian Dominican Sister, theologian, and retreat director who is also very involved in ecumenical dialogue. She is currently doing research on the role of Mary in Islam. Sister Mary Catherine includes the social justice dimension of the Gospel in her work. This concern is evident in her book Mary's Song. *It offers a theological and spiritual reflection on the Magnificat.*

Magnificat! Mary sings forth her gratitude to God. Gratitude is an attitude, a stance toward life. In later life, Mary surely remembered the time of gratitude at the beginning of her motherhood. An attitude of gratitude anchors us in hope that whatever suffering the circumstances of life inflict upon us, all is meaningful in God's regard for us. All has led to the present moment of our lives, and life itself is good.

The astounding courage that comes from a life lived in gratitude was brought home to me one Christmas when I drove through a near blizzard from Detroit to Chicago to visit my family and bring communion from the Christmas liturgy to my ill elderly mother. My heart ached as I entered the nursing home, and my senses were assaulted by the sights, sounds, and smells of the place. My mother's face glowed as she greeted me. My face seemed familiar, but my identity was uncertain. After receiving the eucharist with great devotion, my mother spent some time in prayer. Then, turning to me with a beautiful smile, she told me to always remember to thank God for life's blessings. "God has been so good to us," she said. "Pa used to gather us around his chair and remind us to always remember God's goodness and be grateful." Alzheimer's disease had not obliterated the attitude of gratitude that had permeated my mother's life.

It is not what we do but who we are that is precious in God's sight. What had Mary done to be chosen as mother of the Savior, who was so young, so lowly? "What have I achieved during my lifetime?" is not the appropriate question for the later years of life. Who was Mary that she was chosen? "Who am I at this moment?"—that is the question. It is the quality of love with which we live our lives that is important.

"Hail, favored one!" the angel sang out in greeting Mary. Hail, one already transformed by God's life within. In union with her Creator, Mary became *Theotokos*, "God-bearer." Such mystery is overwhelming. Yet at the time of the annunciation, Mary was transformed by the same Spirit which fell upon the disciples of Jesus at Pentecost and is today present for us. Mary was the first of many believers, first in discipleship, first in love. The great medieval preacher, Meister Eckhart, exhorted all to be "mothers of God."

Mary Catherine Nolan, OP, *Mary's Song*
(Notre Dame, IN: Ave Maria, 2001), 18–19.

The Birth of Jesus

Now this is how the birth of Jesus Christ came about. When his mother Mary was betrothed to Joseph, but before they lived together, she was found with child through the holy Spirit. Joseph her husband, since he was a righteous man, yet unwilling to expose her to shame, decided to divorce her quietly. Such was his intention when, behold, the angel of the Lord appeared to him in a dream and said, "Joseph, son of David, do not be afraid to take Mary your wife into your home. For it is through the holy Spirit that this child has been conceived in her. She will bear a son and you are to name him Jesus, because he will save his people from their sins." All this took place to fulfill what the Lord had said through the prophet:

"Behold, the virgin shall be with child and bear a son,
and they shall name him Emmanuel,"
which means "God is with us."

When Joseph awoke, he did as the angel of the Lord had commanded him and took his wife into his home. He had no relations with her until she bore a son, and he named him Jesus.

When Jesus was born in Bethlehem of Judea, in the days of King Herod, behold, magi from the east arrived in Jerusalem, saying, "Where is the newborn king of the Jews? We saw his star at its rising and have come to do him homage."

When King Herod heard this, he was greatly troubled, and all Jerusalem with him.

Assembling all the chief priests and the scribes of the people, he inquired of them where the Messiah was to be born.

They said to him, "In Bethlehem of Judea, for thus it has been written through the prophet:

'And you, Bethlehem, land of Judah,
are by no means least among the rulers of Judah;
since from you shall come a ruler,
who is to shepherd my people Israel.'"

Then Herod called the magi secretly and ascertained from them the time of the star's appearance. He sent them to Bethlehem and said, "Go and search diligently for the child. When you have found him, bring me word, that I too may go and do him homage." After their audience with the king they set out. And behold, the star that they had seen at its rising preceded them, until it came and stopped over the place where the child was. They were overjoyed at seeing the star, and on entering the house they saw the child with Mary his mother. They prostrated themselves and did him homage. Then they opened their treasures and offered him gifts of gold, frankincense, and myrrh.

And having been warned in a dream not to return to
Herod, they departed for their country by another
way.

MATTHEW 1:18–2:12

In those days a decree went out from Caesar
Augustus that the whole world should be enrolled.
This was the first enrollment, when Quirinius was
governor of Syria. So all went to be enrolled, each to
his own town. And Joseph too went up from Galilee
from the town of Nazareth to Judea, to the city of
David that is called Bethlehem, because he was of the
house and family of David, to be enrolled with Mary,
his betrothed, who was with child. While they were
there, the time came for her to have her child, and she
gave birth to her firstborn son. She wrapped him in
swaddling clothes and laid him in a manger, because
there was no room for them in the inn.

Now there were shepherds in that region living in
the fields and keeping the night watch over their flock.
The angel of the Lord appeared to them and the glory
of the Lord shone around them, and they were struck
with great fear. The angel said to them, "Do not be
afraid; for behold, I proclaim to you good news of
great joy that will be for all the people. For today in the
city of David a savior has been born for you who is
Messiah and Lord. And this will be a sign for you: you
will find an infant wrapped in swaddling clothes and
lying in a manger."

And suddenly there was a multitude of the heavenly host with the angel, praising God and saying:

"Glory to God in the highest
and on earth peace to those on whom his favor
rests."

When the angels went away from them to heaven, the shepherds said to one another, "Let us go, then, to Bethlehem to see this thing that has taken place, which the Lord has made known to us." So they went in haste and found Mary and Joseph, and the infant lying in the manger. When they saw this, they made known the message that had been told them about this child. All who heard it were amazed by what had been told them by the shepherds. And Mary kept all these things, reflecting on them in her heart. Then the shepherds returned, glorifying and praising God for all they had heard and seen, just as it had been told to them.

LUKE 2:1–20

St. Ephrem (c. 306–373), a Syrian deacon and Doctor of the Church, was a prolific writer and perhaps the greatest poet of the Patristic age. His poems and hymns offered a clear apologetic of the Catholic faith against certain Gnostic and Arian heresies of his day. In the excerpts from Hymn XI of his Hymns on the Nativity, *St. Ephrem exercises his poetic imagination as he has the Virgin Mary address her child, Jesus. In Hymn XII, St. Ephrem dwells on Mary's active role in the mystery of the Incarnation.*

Hymn XI.

(The Virgin Mother to Her Child.)

I shall not be jealous, my Son, that Thou art with me, and also with all men. Be Thou God to him that confesses Thee, and be Thou Lord to him that serves Thee, and be Brother to him that loves Thee....

When Thou didst dwell in me, Thou didst also dwell out of me, and when I brought Thee forth openly, Thy hidden might was not removed from me. Thou art within me, and Thou art without me, O Thou that makest Thy Mother amazed....

The Son of the Most High came and dwelt in me, and I became His Mother; and as by a second birth I brought Him forth, so did He bring me forth by the second birth, because He put His Mother's garments on, she clothed her body with His glory....

Hymn XII.

The Babe that I carry carries me, saith Mary, and He has lowered His wings, and taken and placed me between His pinions, and mounted into the air; and a promise has been given me that height and depth shall be my Son's....

In her virginity Eve put on the leaves of shame: Thy Mother put on in her Virginity the garment of Glory that suffices for all. She gave the little vest of the Body to Him that covers all....

St. Ephrem, *Nicene and Post-Nicene Fathers of the Christian Church*, second series, vol. XIII (Grand Rapids, MI: Eerdmans, 1983), 245–46.

St. John of the Cross (1542–1591), the priest, mystic, poet, and Doctor of the Church, worked with St. Teresa of Avila (1515–1582) to reform the Carmelite order and the Church in the sixteenth century. He had a deep personal appreciation for the role of the Virgin Mary in his life, and recognized God's choice of her as the human instrument who freely accepts her mission within the mystery of the Incarnation. The poetry of St. John of the Cross included verses under the title The Romances. *Possibly written during the time of his imprisonment in Toledo in 1578, St. John reflected on the meaning of the Incarnation.*

ROMANCE 8. *THE INCARNATION (continued)*

1. Then He called
The archangel Gabriel
And sent him to
The virgin Mary,

2. At whose consent
The mystery was wrought,
In whom the Trinity
Clothed the Word with flesh.

3. And though Three work this,
It is wrought in the One:
And the Word lived incarnate
In the womb of Mary.

4. And He who had only a Father
Now had a Mother too,
But she was not like others
Who conceive by man.

5. From her own flesh
He received His flesh,
So He is called
Son of God and Son of man.

ROMANCE 9. *The Birth*.

1. When the time had come
For Him to be born
He went forth like the bridegroom
From his bridal chamber,

2. Embracing His bride,
Holding her in His arms,
Whom the gracious Mother
Laid in a manger

3. Among some animals
That were there at that time.
Men sang songs
And angels melodies

4. Celebrating the marriage
Of Two such as these.
But God there in the manger
Cried and moaned;

5. And these tears were jewels
The bride brought to the wedding.
The Mother gazed in sheer wonder
On such an exchange:

6. In God, man's weeping,
And in man, gladness,

To the one and the other
Things usually so strange.

FINIS.

St. John of the Cross, *Romances* 8 and 9, in *The Collected Works of St. John of the Cross*, trans. Kieran Kavanaugh, OCD, and Otilio Rodriguez, OCD (Washington, DC: Institute of Carmelite Studies, 1979), 731–32.

Adrienne von Speyr (1902–1967), born in Switzerland, was a wife, physician, mystic, and author. In 1940, she met the Catholic theologian and then-chaplain at the University of Basel, Father Hans Urs von Balthasar (1905–1988). He received her into the Catholic faith and became her spiritual director and confidant. Many of her written works were the fruit of her intense interior experiences dictated to him. Together they founded a secular institute, the Community of St. John. Her works include a four-volume commentary on St. John's Gospel, works on prayer and the spiritual life, and several books on the Blessed Virgin Mary. The excerpt below on the theme of motherhood is taken from her work Handmaid of the Lord.

Now she carries the Child within her. She carries him physically and spiritually. Physically he develops in her and uses her substance to grow. Spiritually, however, it is more the Child who develops and forms the Mother. In her assent she was ready to become spiritually the Mother of the Lord. In motherhood the Spirit of the Lord takes possession of her in order to make her fruitful in accordance with the Spirit's intention. Thus her motherhood becomes a key to all of Mary's other mysteries. It contains them in itself, as the

Mother has the Son in herself; for all her mysteries have their essence, their core and their solution in the Son. She possesses these mysteries partially, without knowing them in themselves or seeing through them; a comprehensive view is not essential to her task, just as she does not need to understand the Child she is carrying. Her task is to let the mystery happen. Her assent placed her, free, at God's disposal, and in consequence she *has* been disposed of. That she now simply perseveres, that she is the one who lets things happen, is an action which is taken over by grace.

... In Mary this inclusion of the human Yes in the divine Yes is so complete that it flows over upon the saints like a grace peculiarly her own and makes them capable of being indifferent and surrendered in a similar way. When they have given God their consent, they will always be able to do what their mission of the moment requires....

Adrienne von Speyr, Handmaid of the Lord, trans. E. A. Nelson
(San Francisco: Ignatius, 1985), 34–35.

Archbishop Fulton J. Sheen (1895–1979) was a native of El Paso, Illinois. He was ordained to the priesthood for the Diocese of Peoria on September 20, 1919. He taught philosophy at the Catholic University of America, but gained the greatest public recognition as a preacher, author, radio and television evangelist, national Director for the Society of the Propagation of the Faith, and bishop. Sheen served as auxiliary bishop of the Archdiocese of New York (1951–1966), and as the sixth Bishop of the Diocese of Rochester, New York (1966–1969).

His reflection on the role of the Blessed Virgin Mary at the birth of Jesus is found in his very popular Life of Christ.

Out to the hillside to a stable cave, where shepherds sometimes drove their flocks in time of storm, Joseph and Mary went at last for shelter. There, in a place of peace in the lonely abandonment of a cold windswept cave; there, under the floor of the world, He who is born without a mother in heaven, is born without a father on earth.

Of every other child that is born into the world, friends can say that it resembles his mother. This was the first instance in time that anyone could say that the mother resembled the Child. This is the beautiful paradox of the Child Who made His mother; the mother, too, was only a child. It was also the first time in the history of this world that anyone could ever think of heaven as being anywhere else than "somewhere up there"; when the Child was in her arms, Mary now looked down to Heaven.

Fulton J. Sheen, *Life of Christ*
(New York: Doubleday/Image, 1977), 27.

The Presentation of the Lord

When the days were completed for their purification according to the law of Moses, they took him up to Jerusalem to present him to the Lord, just as it is written in the law of the Lord, "Every male that opens the womb shall be consecrated to the Lord," and to offer the sacrifice of "a pair of turtledoves or two young pigeons," in accordance with the dictate in the law of the Lord.

Now there was a man in Jerusalem whose name was Simeon. This man was righteous and devout, awaiting the consolation of Israel, and the holy Spirit was upon him. It had been revealed to him by the holy Spirit that he should not see death before he had seen the Messiah of the Lord. He came in the Spirit into the temple; and when the parents brought in the child Jesus to perform the custom of the law in regard to him, he took him into his arms and blessed God, saying:

> "Now, Master, you may let your servant go
> in peace, according to your word,
> for my eyes have seen your salvation,
> which you prepared in sight of all the peoples,
> a light for revelation to the Gentiles,
> and glory for your people Israel."

The child's father and mother were amazed at what was said about him; and Simeon blessed them and said to Mary his mother, "Behold, this child is destined for the fall and rise of many in Israel, and to be a sign that will be contradicted (and you yourself a sword will pierce) so that the thoughts of many hearts may be revealed." There was also a prophetess, Anna, the daughter of Phanuel, of the tribe of Asher. She was advanced in years, having lived seven years with her husband after her marriage, and then as a widow until she was eighty-four. She never left the temple, but worshiped night and day with fasting and prayer. And coming forward at that very time, she gave thanks to God and spoke about the child to all who were awaiting the redemption of Jerusalem. When they had fulfilled all the prescriptions of the law of the Lord, they returned to Galilee, to their own town of Nazareth. The child grew and became strong, filled with wisdom; and the favor of God was upon him.

LUKE 2:22–40

St. Alphonsus Maria de Liguori (1696–1787) was a lawyer, bishop, theologian, founder of the Congregation of the Most Holy Redeemer (Redemptorists), and Doctor of the Church. Born in the kingdom of Naples, he was a brilliant student who at the age of sixteen received a doctorate in both canon and civil law. In 1726, after several years in the practice of law, he was ordained to the priesthood. He developed a great

love for preaching and enjoyed an exemplary reputation as a confessor. In 1732, he founded the congregation of the Most Holy Savior that became the Congregation of the Most Holy Redeemer. This group of priests and brothers was dedicated to preaching the love of Jesus Christ, especially in missions to people in the countryside. As founder, bishop, and preacher, St. Alphonsus also wrote many works in the areas of morality and spirituality. Blessed Pope Pius IX declared him a doctor of the Church (1871), and Pope Pius XII named him patron of confessors and moral theologians (1950).

In one of his most popular works, The Glories of Mary *(1786), St. Alphonsus desired to promote greater devotion toward the Blessed Virgin Mary and to offer priests an additional resource for their preaching. The work is divided into two main sections. The first section provides a commentary on the Salve Regina. The second part offers sermons on the Marian feasts celebrated throughout the ecclesiastical year, as well as reflections on the sorrows and virtues of Mary.*

In the time of St. Alphonsus, this biblical text was the basis for what was then called the feast of the Purification of Mary. In observance of Jewish law, a woman needed to be purified after childbirth. Mary did not need purification; however, she observed the law. Mary and Joseph bring Jesus to the temple, where they encounter Simeon and Anna. Simeon reveals the universal mission of the child Jesus, and speaks of the "sword" that will pierce Mary's heart. St. Alphonsus reflects on this encounter as an important stage in Mary's participation in the universal sacrificial death of Jesus. He also viewed this text as important in our understanding of the role of Mary's mediation in our salvation.

Let each one, then, consider how much it must have cost Mary, and what strength of mind she had to exercise in this act, by which she sacrificed the life of so amiable a Son to the cross. Behold, therefore, the most fortunate of Mothers, because the Mother of a God; but who was at the same time, of all mothers, the most worthy of compassion, being the most afflicted, inasmuch as she saw her Son destined to the cross from the day on which He was given to her....

Nor did the sufferings of this painful offering end here; nay, even, they only began; for from that time forward, during the whole life of her Son, Mary had constantly before her eyes the death and all the torments which He was to endure....

Mary, then, having by the merit of her sorrows, and by sacrificing her Son, become the Mother of all the redeemed, it is right to believe that through her hands Divine graces, and the means to obtain eternal life, which are the fruits of the merits of Jesus Christ, are given to men. To this it is that St. Bernard alludes when he says, that "when God was about to redeem the human race, He deposited the whole price in Mary's hands"; by which words the Saint gives us to understand that the merits of the Redeemer are applied to our souls by the intercession of the Blessed Virgin; for all graces, which are the fruits of Jesus Christ, were comprised in that price of which she had charge.

PRAYER

O holy Mother of God, and my Mother Mary, you were so deeply interested in my salvation as to offer to death the dearest object of your heart, your beloved Jesus! Since, then, you did so much desire to see me saved, it is right that, after God, I should place all my hopes in you. O yes, most Blessed Virgin, I do indeed entirely confide in you. Ah, by the merit of the great sacrifice which you did offer this day to God, the sacrifice of the life of your Son, entreat Him to have pity on my poor soul, for which this Immaculate Lamb did not refuse to die on the cross.... Ah, my sweetest Mother, for the love of your sacrificed Son, help me always and at all times, and abandon me not. Never permit me to lose by my sins this most amiable Redeemer, whom on this day you did offer with such bitter grief to the cruel death of the cross. Remind Him that I am your servant, that in you I have placed all my hope; say, at the end, that you desire my salvation, and He will certainly graciously hear you.

St. Alphonsus Maria de Liguori, *The Glories of Mary*, 2nd ed. (London: Burns, Oates & Washbourne, 1868), 363–64, 366–67, 370.

The Finding of Jesus in the Temple

Each year his parents went to Jerusalem for the feast of Passover, and when he was twelve years old, they went up according to festival custom. After they had completed its days, as they were returning, the boy Jesus remained behind in Jerusalem, but his parents did not know it. Thinking that he was in the caravan, they journeyed for a day and looked for him among their relatives and acquaintances, but not finding him, they returned to Jerusalem to look for him. After three days they found him in the temple, sitting in the midst of the teachers, listening to them and asking them questions, and all who heard him were astounded at his understanding and his answers. When his parents saw him, they were astonished, and his mother said to him, "Son, why have you done this to us? Your father and I have been looking for you with great anxiety." And he said to them, "Why were you looking for me? Did you not know that I must be in my Father's house?" But they did not understand what he said to them. He went down with them and came to Nazareth, and was obedient to them; and his mother kept all these things in her heart. And Jesus advanced (in) wisdom and age and favor before God and man.

Luke 2:41–52

Pope John Paul II offered the Church and the world a rich understanding of the role of the Blessed Virgin Mary in the economy of salvation. His corpus of Marian theology and spirituality, rooted in his personal experience and life of prayer, include his writings, speeches delivered to various groups when he traveled around the world, and a series of Wednesday general audience talks that he presented from September 1995 to November 1997.

On January 15, 1997, he reflected on the dialogue recorded between Mary and Joseph and twelve-year-old Jesus after they had been separated from each other on the occasion of the Holy Family's pilgrimage to Jerusalem. Eventually, Joseph and Mary find Jesus in the temple "sitting in the midst of the teachers" (Lk 2:46). The Pope's reflection:

Through this episode, Jesus prepared his Mother for the mystery of the redemption. During those three dramatic days when the Son withdrew from them to stay in the Temple, Mary and Joseph experienced an anticipation of the Triduum of Jesus' passion, death and resurrection....

Revealing a wisdom that amazed his listeners, he began to practice the art of dialogue that would be a characteristic of his saving mission. His Mother asked Jesus: "Son, why have you treated us so? Behold your father and I have been looking for you anxiously" (Lk 2:48). Here we can discern an echo of the "whys" asked by so many mothers about the suffering their children cause them, as well as the questions welling up in the heart of every man and woman in times of trial.

In the form of a question, Jesus' reply is highly significant: "How is it that you sought me? Did you not know that I must be in my Father's house?" (Lk 2:49). With this response, he disclosed the mystery of his person to Mary and Joseph in an unexpected, unforeseen way, inviting them to go beyond appearances and unfolding before them new horizons for his future. In his reply to his anguished Mother, the Son immediately revealed the reason for his behavior. Mary had said: "Your father," indicating Joseph; Jesus replied: "My Father," meaning the heavenly Father....

With this attitude, Jesus intended to reveal the mysterious aspects of his intimacy with the Father, aspects which Mary intuited without knowing how to associate them with the trial she was undergoing.

Luke's words teach us how Mary lived in the depths of her being this truly unusual episode. She "kept all these things in her heart" (Lk 2:51). The Mother of Jesus associated these events with the mystery of her Son, revealed to her at the annunciation. She pondered them in the silence of contemplation, offering her cooperation in the spirit of a renewed "*fiat.*" In this way the first link was forged in a chain of events that would gradually lead Mary beyond the natural role deriving from her motherhood, to put herself at the service of her divine Son's mission.

At the Temple in Jerusalem, in this prelude to his saving mission, Jesus associated his Mother with himself. No longer was she merely the one who gave him birth, but the woman who through her own obedience to the Father's plan can cooperate in the mystery of redemption. Thus keeping in her heart an event so charged with meaning, Mary attained a new dimension of her cooperation in salvation.

Pope John Paul II, *Theotokos. Woman,*
Mother, Disciple: A Catechesis on Mary, Mother of God.
(Boston: Pauline Books & Media, 2000), pp. 165–68.

The Hidden Life

He went down with them and came to Nazareth, and was obedient to them; and his mother kept all these things in her heart. And Jesus advanced [in] wisdom and age and favor before God and man.

LUKE 2:51–52

St. Paul teaches us "your life is hidden with Christ in God" (Col 3:3). The Gospel gives little indication of the life of the Holy Family in Nazareth before the public ministry of Jesus began. This life has captured the imagination of artists and scholars and is found in the early church noncanonical writings known as the apocryphal literature. In January 1964, on the occasion of his visit to the Holy Land, Pope Paul VI (1964–1978) spoke on the significance of Nazareth as a model school for growth in the Christian life.

How I would like to return to my childhood and attend the simple yet profound school that is Nazareth! How wonderful to be close to Mary, learning again the lesson of the true meaning of life, learning again God's truths....

Pope Paul VI, "Nazareth, a Model," in *The Liturgy of the Hours*, Vol. I (New York: Catholic Book Publishing Co., 1975), 427.

Blessed Abbot Columba Marmion, OSB (1858–1923), birth name Joseph, was the son of an Irish father and a French mother. In 1881, after having completed his theological studies at the College of the Propagation of the Faith in Rome, Joseph Marmion was ordained a priest for the Archdiocese of Dublin, Ireland. He served as a parish priest, professor at the seminary in Clonliffe, and as a spiritual director at a prison before he discerned his call to serve God and the Church as a Benedictine monk in the abbey of Maredsous, Belgium. He served as abbot from 1909 until his death in 1923. He was recognized as a holy priest and a very popular spiritual director, writer, and teacher. Abbot Marmion was also very enthusiastic in his promotion of vocations to the priesthood and the religious life. Pope John Paul II beatified Abbot Marmion during the Jubilee Year 2000.

In one of Abbot Marmion's classic works, Christ in His Mysteries, *Marmion reflected on the life of the Blessed Virgin Mary at Nazareth before the public ministry of Jesus.*

It is especially through the Blessed Virgin Mary that we shall obtain a share in the graces that Christ merited for us by His hidden life at Nazareth. Those years must have been for the Mother of God a wellspring of priceless graces. We are dazzled by the very thought of them, and intuitions scarcely to be expressed in words are awakened within us when we reflect upon what those thirty years must have been for Mary and how every movement, word and action of Jesus were for her as so many revelations.

Doubtless there must have been much that was incomprehensible even for the Blessed Virgin. No one could live in continual contact, as she did, with the Infinite, without at times feeling and touching mystery. But yet what abundant light for her soul, what a continual increase of love this ineffable intercourse with a God, working under her eyes, must have wrought in her immaculate heart.

Mary lived with Jesus in a union surpassing all that can be said of it. They were truly one; the mind, heart, soul, in a word the whole existence of the Virgin-Mother was in absolute accord with the mind, heart, soul and life of her Son. Her life was, as it were, a pure and perfect vibration, tranquil and full of love, of the very life of Jesus.

What was the source of this union and of this love in Mary? It was her faith. The Blessed Virgin's faith is one of her most characteristic virtues.

How wondrous and how full of confidence is her faith in the word of the Angel! The heavenly messenger announces to her an unheard of mystery which astonishes and overthrows nature: the conception of a God in a virginal womb. And Mary says: *Fiat mihi secundum verbum tuum* [Lk 1:38— May it be done to me according to your word]. It is because she gives the full assent of her mind to the Word of the Angel that she merits to become the Mother of the Incarnate Word....

Mary's faith in the Divinity of Jesus is never shaken. She ever sees in her Son the Infinite God.

And yet to what trials is not this faith subjected! Her Son is God. The Angel tells her that Jesus will sit in the throne of David, that He will save the world, and of His kingdom there shall be no end. And Simeon predicts to her that Jesus will be a sign of contradiction, a cause of ruin as well as of salvation. Then Mary has to flee into Egypt to snatch her Son from Herod's tyrannical fury; until He is thirty years old, her son, Who is God and comes to redeem the human race, lives, in a poor workshop, a life of labour, submission and obscurity. Later on, she will see her Son pursued by the hatred of the Pharisees, she will see Him forsaken by His disciples, in the hands of His enemies, she will see Him hanging upon the Cross, mocked and despised, she will hear Him cry out from the depths of anguish: "My God, my God, why hast thou forsaken me"—but her faith will remain unshaken. It is even then, at the foot of the Cross, that it shines in all its splendour. Mary ever recognizes her Son as her God, and therefore the Church proclaims her "the Faithful Virgin" supereminently: *Virgo fidelis*.

And this faith is the source of Mary's love for her Son; it is through this faith that she remains ever united to Jesus. Let us ask her to obtain for us a firm and practical faith that has its culmination in love and in the accomplishment of the Divine will: "Behold the handmaid of the Lord, be it done to me according to Thy word." These words sum up all Mary's existence. May they likewise sum up ours.

Dom Columba Marmion, *Christ in His Mysteries*,
trans. Mother M. St. Thomas of Tyburn Convent
(St. Louis, MO: B. Herder Book Co., 1939), 170–72.

St. Peter Julian Eymard (1811–1868) was ordained to the priesthood in 1834 for the Diocese of Grenoble, France. In the early nineteenth century, French society deeply felt the impact of the French Revolution. The rigoristic spirituality of Jansenism also spread widely, emphasizing the

sinful condition and unworthiness of all human beings. This caused many Catholics to stay away from receiving Holy Communion because they thought they were so unworthy.

From his childhood, Peter Julian Eymard cultivated a strong devotion to Jesus in the Eucharist. He also had a strong devotion to the Blessed Virgin Mary, one that grew through his pilgrimages to various Marian shrines in France. In 1839, he joined the religious community of the Marists. In 1856, notwithstanding several obstacles and even opposition, he founded the Congregation of the Blessed Sacrament. The community opened its first house in Paris. Two years later, together with Marguerite Guillot, he founded the Servants of the Blessed Sacrament for women. The letters, conferences, and written works of Eymard present God's overwhelming love for all people. This love is most perfectly and dramatically found in the eucharistic presence of Jesus. Contemplation of this love motivates the adorer of the Blessed Sacrament to address the major concerns of society.

Blessed Pope John XXIII canonized St. Peter Julian Eymard on December 9, 1962. Eymard has received the title of "Apostle of the Eucharist." The Eymard library includes nine small volumes of his conferences, talks, and writings around various spiritual themes. In his work Our Lady of the Blessed Sacrament, *the chapter "The Interior Life of Mary" develops Eymard's understanding of the hidden spiritual life of the Blessed Virgin Mary. For Eymard, the cultivation of a deeply personal interior life is intimately connected to the apostolate. Only in the discovery of the interior does one "enjoy God's presence."*

Her life was passed in silence and obscurity, and the Gospel narrative says nothing about it. This was because Mary was to be an illustrious model of the hidden life—a life hidden with God in Jesus Christ—a life which we should strive to honor and faithfully copy in our conduct....

Hence I say, if we wish to become saints, we must become interior souls. We are obliged thereto by our vocation as adorers. Without this interior spirit, how can we pray? If in the presence of our Lord we cannot spend a single instant without a book, if we have nothing to say to Him from our own heart, what are we going to do at adoration? What! Can we never speak to Him from the abundance of our own heart? Must we always borrow the thoughts and words of strangers? No, no! Let us strive to become recollected, interior souls. No one can be this in the way that Jesus and Mary were; but everyone can become recollected in the degree given him by grace. Without the interior life, we shall never receive any consolation, encouragement in prayer....

We should talk to our Lord when kneeling in His presence, ask Him questions, await His reply: we should enjoy God's presence. We should be happy in His company, happy in His service; we should take pleasure in His familiarity, so sweet, so encouraging. But to discover the Heart of Jesus we must be interior.

St. Peter Juliam Eymard, *Our Lady of the Blessed Sacrament* (Cleveland, OH: Emmanuel Publications, 1930), 54, 55, 56.

The Wedding Feast at Cana

On the third day there was a wedding in Cana in Galilee, and the mother of Jesus was there. Jesus and his disciples were also invited to the wedding. When the wine ran short, the mother of Jesus said to him, "They have no wine." (And) Jesus said to her, "Woman, how does your concern affect me? My hour has not yet come." His mother said to the servers, "Do whatever he tells you." Now there were six stone water jars there for Jewish ceremonial washings, each holding twenty to thirty gallons. Jesus told them, "Fill the jars with water." So they filled them to the brim. Then he told them, "Draw some out now and take it to the head-waiter." So they took it. And when the headwaiter tasted the water that had become wine, without knowing where it came from (although the servers who had drawn the water knew), the headwaiter called the bridegroom and said to him, "Everyone serves good wine first, and then when people have drunk freely, an inferior one; but you have kept the good wine until now." Jesus did this as the beginning of his signs in Cana in Galilee and so revealed his glory, and his disciples began to believe in him.

After this, he and his mother, (his) brothers, and his disciples went down to Capernaum and stayed there only a few days.

JOHN 2:1–12

In his work Seven Words of Jesus and Mary: Lessons from Cana and Calvary, *Archbishop Fulton J. Sheen reflects on the message to be found when one considers the seven recorded times that the Blessed Mother spoke in the Gospels, and the seven recorded words of Jesus from the cross. Sheen identifies the sixth word as "the hour." It links Mary's words at Cana, "They have no wine" (Jn 2:3) with Jesus' words, "It is finished" (Jn 19:30).*

When Mary at the foot of the cross saw that soldier offer him wine and heard him say, "It is consummated," she thought of the moment when it all began. There was wine there too, but not enough. It was the marriage feast of Cana. When in the course of the banquet the wine gave out, the first to observe the lack of wine was not the steward. It was Our Blessed Mother. She notes human needs even before those commissioned to supply them.

Our Blessed Mother said to Our Lord a simple prayer: "They have no wine" (Jn 2:3). That was all. And her Son answered: "Woman." He did not call her Mother.... Why "Woman"? He was equivalently saying to her: "Mary, you are my mother. You are asking me to begin my public life, to declare myself the Messiah, the Son of God, by working my first miracle. The moment I do that first miracle you cease to be just my mother. As I reveal myself as Redeemer, you become in a certain sense a co-redemptrix, the mother of all men. That is why I address you by the title of universal motherhood: It will be the beginning of your womanhood."

But what did he mean by saying: "My hour is not yet come?" Our Blessed Lord used that word *hour* often in relation to his Passion and Death.... The hour meant the cross.

The working of his first miracle was the beginning of the hour. His Sixth Word from the cross was the end of that hour. The Passion was finished. The water had been changed into wine; the wine into blood. It is perfected. The work is done.

From these words the lesson emerges that, between the beginning of our assigned duties and their completion and perfection, there intervenes an "hour," or a moment of mortification, sacrifice, and death. No life is ever finished without it. Between the Cana when we launch the vocation of our lives, and that moment of triumph when we can say we succeeded, there must come the interval of the cross. Our Lord could have had no other motive in asking us to take up our cross daily than to perfect ourselves. It was almost like saying, between the day you begin to be a concert pianist and the day you triumph in concert work, there must come the "hour" of hard study, dull exercises, and painful addiction to work.

Fulton J. Sheen, *Seven Words of Jesus and Mary: Lessons from Cana and Calvary* (Liguori, MO: Liguori/Triumph, 2001), 78–79.

"Who Is My Mother?"

Then his mother and his brothers came to him, but they could not reach him because of the crowd. And he was told, "Your mother and your brothers are standing outside, wanting to see you." But he said to them, "My mother and my brothers are those who hear the word of God and do it."[*]

LUKE 8:19–21

St. Augustine (354–430), bishop, theologian, mystic, and Doctor of the Church, wrote his treatise on Holy Virginity *(c. 401) as a companion work to his treatise on* The Excellence of Marriage. *His commentary on Matthew 12:46–50 follows.*

It is written in the gospel that when a message was brought to Christ that his mother and brothers, that is his relatives by birth, were waiting outside unable to come nearer

---

[*] In the Gospels, the greatest form of intimacy and "privilege" with Jesus consisted in doing the will of his Father. All other relationships, even family relationships, were of secondary importance (Mt 12:46–50; Mk 3:31–35; Lk 8:19-21; Lk 11:27–28).

because of the crowd, he answered, *"Who is my mother? Who are my brothers?" And stretching his hands out over his disciples, he said, "These are my brothers"; and then, "Whoever does my Father's will, that person is my brother and mother and sister"* (Mt 12: 48–50). What was he teaching us other than to value our spiritual family more highly than relationship by birth, and that what makes people blessed is not being close to upright and holy persons by blood relationship, but being united with them by obeying and imitating their doctrine and way of life. It was a greater blessing for Mary, therefore, to receive Christ's faith than to conceive his flesh.... Finally, what advantage was that relationship for his brothers and sisters, that is those related to him by birth, who did not believe in him? So even the close relationship of being his mother would have been no benefit to Mary, if she had not carried Christ in her heart, a greater privilege than doing so in her body.

St. Augustine, *Holy Virginity* 3, in *The Works of St. Augustine*, ed. John E. Rotelle, OSA, trans. Ray Kearney, vol. IX (Hyde Park, NY: New City Press, 1999), 69.

Mary at the Foot of the Cross

Standing by the cross of Jesus were his mother and his mother's sister, Mary the wife of Clopas, and Mary of Magdala. When Jesus saw his mother and the disciple there whom he loved, he said to his mother, "Woman, behold, your son." Then he said to the disciple, "Behold, your mother." And from that hour the disciple took her into his home.

JOHN 19:25–27

Hans Urs von Balthasar (1905–1988), born in Switzerland, was one of the most distinguished Catholic theologians and prolific writers of the twentieth century. In 1929, von Balthasar entered a Jesuit novitiate. In 1936, following his study of philosophy at Pullach near Munich, and his study of theology at Fourviere near Lyons, France, von Balthasar was ordained a priest for the Society of Jesus. In 1940, as a student chaplain at the University of Basel, Balthasar met Adrienne von Speyr (1902–1967) and became her spiritual director. She was a medical doctor and a Protestant. Following the death of her first husband, she married Werner Kaegi. Balthasar received her into the Catholic Church. On the basis of her mystical experiences and visions, she dictated to Balthasar many of her published volumes. Balthasar claimed that their work was inseparable, and he credited her with an enormous influence

over his own writing. Together they founded the secular institute of the Community of St. John. To collaborate with Adrienne von Speyr in her "mission," Balthasar left the Society of Jesus. He was later incardinated into the Swiss diocese of Chur. Pope John Paul II renewed Pope Paul VI's appointment of Balthasar to the International Theological Commission. In 1988, Pope John Paul II named Balthasar to the College of Cardinals. However, he died just three days before coming to Rome for the ceremony. Cardinal Joseph Ratzinger preached the homily at his funeral Mass.

Balthasar believed that our response to the drama of God's self-disclosure of beauty, truth, and goodness located in the person of Jesus Christ was fundamentally found in the personal and ecclesial fiat of the Blessed Virgin Mary. Mary's fiat at the moment of the annunciation reaches a dramatic threshold at the foot of the cross. Balthasar writes:

Beneath the Cross, her consent becomes the most excruciating affirmation of her Son's sacrifice. We have already seen in some detail how the Mother's Yes crowns that process of heightening that affects the entirety of Old Testament faith; it gives birth to ecclesial faith and is its pattern. Insofar as Mary's Yes is one of the presuppositions of the Son's Incarnation, it can be, beneath the Cross, a constituent part of his sacrifice. It is not, of course, of equal significance.... Here, therefore, he makes room for his Mother's part, so different and so painful, which is simply to let his suffering happen and to accept all the pain that must happen to her too. Mary allows the Cross to take place: this is the archetype of the Church's entire faith, which "allows things to take place"; this is seen particularly in the event of the Eucharist, that existentially perfect and exemplary gesture that is implanted into the Church and handed on down the centuries. Here, and here alone, we discern that this "letting be" is also a sacrifice ...

that is, the most painful renunciation and forfeiting of something.... Only where there is the free-will transferring of
something from one's own possession to the realm of the
divine can we speak of sacrifice....

Christ is entrusted to the hands of Mary at birth and at
his death: this is more central than his being given into the
hands of the Church in her official, public aspect. The former is the precondition for the latter. Before the masculine,
official side appears in the Church, the Church as the
woman, the helpmate of the Man, is already there. And it is
only possible for the presbyters to exercise their office in the
Church of the Incarnate, Crucified and Risen One if they are
sustained by the "supra-official" Woman who cherishes and
nurtures this official side; for she alone utters the Yes that is
necessary if the Incarnation of the Word is to take place. It is
from this archetypal Yes that the faith—more or less weak,
more or less strong—of the other members of the Church is
nourished.... It is from this archetypal Yes that believers, in
the celebration of the Eucharist, draw their loving resolve—
more or less consciously—to let God's will happen, painful
though it may be, since his will is for the salvation of the
world and the Church.

Hans Urs von Balthasar, *Theo-Drama*, trans. Graham Harrison, vol. IV
(San Francisco: Ignatius Press, 1994), 395, 396, 397, 398.

In his encyclical Redemptoris Mater (Mother of the Redeemer),
Pope John Paul II viewed Mary's presence at the foot of the cross as the

culmination of her role in the mystery of salvation. He also developed the idea that this scene forms the basis for all Christians to entrust themselves to the ongoing maternal mediation of the Blessed Virgin.

She [Mary] cooperated, as the Second Vatican Council teaches, with a maternal love. Here we perceive the real value of the words spoken by Jesus to his Mother at the hour of the Cross: "Woman, behold your son" and to the disciple: "Behold your mother" (Jn 19:26–27). They are words which determine *Mary's place in the life of Christ's disciples* and they express—as I have already said—the new motherhood of the Mother of the Redeemer: a spiritual motherhood, born from the heart of the Paschal Mystery of the Redeemer of the world. It is a motherhood in the order of grace, for it implores the gift of the Spirit, who raises up the new children of God, redeemed through the sacrifice of Christ: that Spirit whom Mary too, together with the Church, received on the day of Pentecost.

Her motherhood is particularly noted and experienced by the Christian people at the *Sacred Banquet*—the liturgical celebration of the mystery of the Redemption—at which Christ, his *true body born of the Virgin Mary*, becomes present.

The piety of the Christian people has always very rightly sensed a *profound link* between devotion to the Blessed Virgin and worship of the Eucharist: this is a fact that can be seen in both the liturgy of the West and the East, in the traditions of the Religious Families, in the modern movements of spirituality, including those for youth, and in the pastoral practice of the Marian Shrines. *Mary guides the faithful to the Eucharist.*

Of the essence of motherhood is the fact that it concerns the person. Motherhood always establishes a *unique and unrepeatable relationship* between two people: *between mother and child* and *between child and mother*. Even when the same woman is the mother of many children, her personal relationship with each one of them is of the very essence of motherhood. For each child is generated in a unique and unrepeatable way, and this is true both for the mother and for the child. Each child is surrounded in the same way by that maternal love on which are based the child's development and coming to maturity as a human being.

It can be said that motherhood "in the order of grace" preserves the analogy with what "in the order of nature" characterizes the union between mother and child. In the light of this fact it becomes easier to understand why in Christ's testament on Golgotha his Mother's new motherhood is expressed in the singular, in reference to one man: "Behold your Son."

It can also be said that these same words fully show the reason *for the Marian dimension of the life of Christ's disciples.* This is true not only of John, who at that hour stood at the foot of the Cross together with his Master's Mother, but it is also true of every disciple of Christ, of every Christian. The Redeemer entrusts his mother to the disciple, and at the same time he gives her to him as his mother. Mary's motherhood, which becomes man's inheritance, is a gift: *a gift which Christ himself makes* personally to every individual. The Redeemer entrusts Mary to John because he entrusts John to Mary. At the foot of the Cross there begins that special *entrusting of humanity to the Mother of Christ*, which in the history of the Church has been practiced and expressed in different ways. The same Apostle and Evangelist, after reporting the words addressed by Jesus on the Cross to his Mother and to himself, adds: "And from that hour the disciple took her to his own home" (Jn 19:27). This statement certainly means that the role of the son was attributed to the disciple and that he assumed responsibility for the Mother of his beloved Master. And since Mary was given as a mother to him personally, the statement indicates, even though indirectly, everything expressed by the intimate relationship of a child with its mother. And all of this can be included in the word "entrusting." Such entrusting is *the response* to a person's love, and in particular *to the love of a mother*.

The Marian dimension of the life of a disciple of Christ is expressed in a special way precisely through this filial entrusting to the Mother of Christ, which began with the testament of the Redeemer on Golgotha. Entrusting himself to Mary in a filial manner, the Christian, like the Apostle John, "welcomes" the Mother of Christ "into his own home" and brings her into everything that makes up his inner life, that is to say into his human and Christian "I": he *"took her to his own home."* Thus the Christian seeks to be taken into that "maternal charity" with which the Redeemer's Mother "cares for the brethren of her Son," in whose birth and development she cooperates" in the measure of the gift proper to each one through the power of Christ's Spirit. Thus also is exercised that motherhood in the Spirit which became Mary's role at the foot of the Cross and in the Upper Room.

Pope John Paul II, *Redemptoris Mater*, nos. 44 and 45.

At the Cenacle

When they entered the city they went to the upper room where they were staying, Peter and John and James and Andrew, Philip and Thomas, Bartholomew and Matthew, James son of Alphaeus, Simon the Zealot, and Judas son of James. All these devoted themselves with one accord to prayer, together with some women, and Mary the mother of Jesus, and his brothers.

ACTS OF THE APOSTLES 1:13–14

In his encyclical letter Ecclesia de Eucharistia (On the Eucharist in Its Relationship to the Church), *Pope John Paul II writes:*

If we wish to rediscover in all its richness the profound relationship between the Church and the Eucharist, we cannot neglect Mary, Mother and model of the Church.... Mary can guide us toward this most holy sacrament, because she herself has a profound relationship with it.

At first glance, the Gospel is silent on this subject. The account of the institution of the Eucharist on the night of

Holy Thursday makes no mention of Mary. Yet we know that she was present among the apostles who prayed "with one accord" (cf. Acts 1:14) *in the first community which gathered after the Ascension in expectation of Pentecost.* Certainly Mary must have been present at the Eucharistic celebrations of the first generations of Christians, who were devoted to "the breaking of bread" (Acts 2:42).

Pope John Paul II, *Ecclesia de Eucharistia*
(Boston: Pauline Books & Media, 2003), no. 53.

The nineteenth-century founder of the Congregation of the Blessed Sacrament, St. Peter Julian Eymard, who considered the possibility of opening one of his religious houses at the Cenacle in Jerusalem, wrote:

Let us follow our Mother to the Cenacle and listen to the lessons that she there teaches us, lessons that she has received from her Divine Son, with whom she conversed day and night. She is the faithful echo of His Heart and of His love. Let us love Mary tenderly; let us labor under her maternal eye, and pray by her side. Let us be her truly devoted children, for by so doing, we shall honor Jesus who has given her to us for our Mother, that she may teach us how to love Him by the example of her own life.

Honor in Mary, at the foot of the Tabernacle, all the mysteries of her life, for all these were stations, as it were, leading to the Cenacle. In Mary's life there you will find the model and the consolation of your own life. In the Cenacle, this august Queen kneels as adoratrix and servant of the Most Blessed Sacrament: kneel at your Mother's side and pray with her, and in so doing, you will continue her Eucharistic life on earth.

St. Peter Julian Eymard,
Our Lady of the Blessed Sacrament, 104, 105.

Blessed Pope John XXIII (1958–1963) convoked the Second Vatican Council (1962–1965). In September 1961, he published an apostolic letter on the Holy Rosary. At the conclusion of the letter, he added a series of meditations on the mysteries of the Rosary. His meditation on the Third Glorious Mystery, the descent of the Holy Spirit upon the Apostles on the first Pentecost, links the Blessed Mother to the earliest moments of the history of the Church.

At the Last Supper the apostles received the promise of the Spirit; later, in that very room, in the absence of Jesus but in the presence of Mary, they received him as Christ's supreme gift. Indeed, what is his spirit if not the Consoler and Giver of life to men? The Holy Spirit is continually poured out on the Church and within it every day; all ages and all men belong to the Spirit, belong to the Church. The Church's triumphs are not always externally visible, but they are always there and always rich in surprises, often in miracles.

The Hail Marys of the present mystery have a special intention during this year of great enthusiasm when the whole Holy Church, a pilgrim on this earth, is preparing for the Ecumenical Council. The Council must succeed in being a new Pentecost of faith, of the apostolate, of extraordinary graces for the welfare of men, and the peace of the world. Mary the Mother of Jesus, always our own sweet Mother, was with the apostles in the upper room for the miracle of Pentecost. Let us keep closer to her in our rosary, all this year. Our prayers, united with hers, will renew the miracle of old. It will be like the rising of a new day, a radiant dawn for the Catholic Church, holy and growing ever more holy, Catholic and growing ever more Catholic, in these modern days.

Pope John XXIII, "The Holy Rosary," in *Journal of a Soul*,
trans. Dorothy White (New York: Signet, 1966), 427.

The Woman of the Apocalypse

A great sign appeared in the sky, a woman clothed with the sun, with the moon under her feet, and on her head a crown of twelve stars. She was with child and wailed aloud in pain as she labored to give birth. Then another sign appeared in the sky; it was a huge red dragon, with seven heads and ten horns, and on its heads were seven diadems. Its tail swept away a third of the stars in the sky and hurled them down to the earth. Then the dragon stood before the woman about to give birth, to devour her child when she gave birth. She gave birth to a son, a male child, destined to rule all the nations with an iron rod. Her child was caught up to God and his throne. The woman herself fled into the desert where she had a place prepared by God, that there she might be taken care of for twelve hundred and sixty days.

Then war broke out in heaven; Michael and his angels battled against the dragon. The dragon and its angels fought back, but they did not prevail and there was no longer any place for them in heaven. The huge dragon, the ancient serpent, who is called the Devil and Satan, who deceived the whole world, was thrown down to earth, and its angels were thrown down with it.

Then I heard a loud voice in heaven say:

"Now have salvation and power come,
and the kingdom of our God
and the authority of his Anointed.
For the accuser of our brothers is cast out,
who accuses them before our God day and night.
They conquered him by the blood of the Lamb
and by the word of their testimony;
love for life did not deter them from death.
Therefore, rejoice, you heavens,
and you who dwell in them.
But woe to you, earth and sea,
for the Devil has come down to you in great fury,
for he knows he has but a short time."

When the dragon saw that it had been thrown down to the earth, it pursued the woman who had given birth to the male child. But the woman was given the two wings of the great eagle, so that she could fly to her place in the desert, where, far from the serpent, she was taken care of for a year, two years, and a half-year. The serpent, however, spewed a torrent of water out of his mouth after the woman to sweep her away with the current. But the earth helped the woman and opened its mouth and swallowed the flood that the dragon spewed out of its mouth. Then the dragon became angry with the woman and went off to wage war against the rest of her offspring, those who keep God's commandments and bear witness to Jesus. It took its position on the sand of the sea.

REVELATION 12:1–18

Mary and the Church are at work in every soul. All the time Christ on earth is being born, attacked and yet glorified. Yet all this lies hidden behind a humiliating exterior. But it is all there in reality, the new birth into eternity, the sun of the risen Lord. Let us therefore look to her, the noble Lady, our Mother Mary, our mother the Church: let us turn lovingly to the sorrowful mother of our life in Christ....

Thus is Mary, and with her the Church, our consolation in suffering in our spiritual lives, which here on earth seem to be but daily dying; our assurance also of the bright morning of eternity to come, of which already in our hearts we can discern the faintest dawn. Yes, indeed we are already clothed with the sun, and the moon of passing things is already under our feet, "until the day dawn, and the day-star arise in our hearts" (2 Pet 1:19). As long as it is still night, let us look to the woman with the moon under her feet, for in her all is done, that with us is still to come. For this woman stands for the Church. Yet we can also see in her the Blessed Mary, for

she is the mother of the Church, since she gave birth to him
who is the head of the Church.

Hugo Rahner, SJ, *Our Lady and the Church*,
trans. Sebastian Bullough, OP
(New York: Pantheon/Random, 1961), 113–15.

*Scott Hahn (1957–) is a Catholic theologian, author, and apologist.
Formerly a Protestant, Hahn had extensive pastoral experience with
Protestant congregations in several states. He entered the Catholic
Church at the Easter Vigil in 1986. He earned a PhD in biblical theology from Marquette University in 1995. His wife, Kimberly, entered the
Catholic Church at Easter in 1990. Their conversion experience is
described in their book* Rome Sweet Home: Our Journey to Catholicism *(San Francisco: Ignatius, 1993). He is currently a professor of theology and scripture at Franciscan University of Steubenville, and
founder and director of the St. Paul Center for Biblical Theology. In
2005, he was appointed as the Pope Benedict XVI Chair of Biblical
Theology and Liturgical Proclamation at St. Vincent Seminary in
Latrobe, Pennsylvania.*

In his work Hail Holy Queen: The Mother of God in the Word
of God, *Hahn reflects on the image of the woman of the apocalypse.*

The woman of the Apocalypse is the ark of the covenant in the heavenly temple; and that woman is the Virgin
Mary.... In the fourth century, for example, Saint Ambrose
saw the woman clearly as the Virgin Mary, "because she is
mother of the Church, for she brought forth Him who is the
Head of the Church"; yet Ambrose also saw Revelation's

woman as an allegory of the Church herself.... Saint Augustine, too, held that the woman of the Apocalypse "signifies Mary, who, being spotless, brought forth our spotless Head. Who herself also showed forth in herself a figure of holy Church, so that as she in bringing forth a Son remained a virgin so the Church also should during the whole of time be bringing forth His members, and yet not lose her virgin estate."

As Mary birthed Christ to the world, so the Church births believers, "other Christs," to each generation. As the Church becomes mother to believers in baptism, so Mary becomes mother to believers as brothers of Christ.

Scott Hahn, *Hail Holy Queen: The Mother of God in the Word of God* (New York: Doubleday, 2001), 65–66.

Mary, Mother of Holiness: A Prayer

I will greatly rejoice in the Lord,
  my whole being shall exult in my God;
for he has clothed me with the garments of
    salvation,
  he has covered me with the robe of righteous-
    ness,
as a bridegroom decks himself with a garland,
  and as a bride adorns herself with her jewels.

ISAIAH 61:10

The Most Reverend William Giaquinta (1914–1994) was the founder of the Pro Sanctity Movement, a lay ecclesial movement that promotes the universal call to holiness for all people. Ordained to the priesthood in 1939 for the Diocese of Rome, he was appointed bishop of Tivoli in 1968. He spent his life promoting the interior life and the call to holiness. In 2004, he was declared Servant of God. He founded two Secular Institutes (the Apostolic Oblates for consecrated and committed lay-women, and the Apostolic Sodales for priests), as well as three ecclesial groups (the Priestly Movement, the Social Animators for laymen, and the Pro Sanctity Movement). All are dedicated to the promotion of the universal call to holiness. This selection is one of his many prayers and

spiritual writings. It calls us to join our hearts to Mary, who remained near Christ and shows us the way to holiness.

MARY, MOTHER OF HOLINESS

All beautiful are you, O Mary,
and original sin is not in you.
You are immaculate, all holy.
Thus the Archangel Gabriel contemplated you,
and to you, full of grace,
he revealed the sacred mystery of redemption.

From you, immaculate and holy,
what else could the world receive
but the one who is all-holy?

The Spirit of love formed him
in your immaculate womb,
overshadowing you with the mystery of his presence.
And through the almighty arm of him,
whose name is holy,
you brought forth in humanity him who,
being God by nature,
became man for the salvation
and sanctification of the world.

While he was growing in wisdom, age, and grace,
you foresaw the altar prepared for his holocaust.
Discreet, you followed him
to the mountain of beatitudes,
gleaning from his lips
the invitation to walk towards the perfection
of the Father

and to draw from him the living water of grace,
which he came to bring to us in abundance.

You did not leave Jesus
when they crucified him on Calvary,
meriting for humanity the strength to do penance
and to become holy.

At the foot of the Cross, mother of the first Martyr,
you became mother of those who,
by shedding their blood,
would testify heroically to their love for your Son.

Proclaimed mother of John,
you also became mother of those
who would witness to their love by holiness of life.

While anxiously awaiting the Sanctifier,
who was to flood the hearts of the Apostles,
gathered so close to you, Mother,
you implored for them the gift of holiness.

Crowned Queen of saints by him who is all holy,
in heaven you continue your work of intercession
and sanctification.

To you we turn, holy Mary,
mother of us who are not yet holy.
Grant us love for your Son,
the joy of the Spirit,
a longing for the perfection of the Father,
and the hope that we, too,
will join you in the land of saints.
Amen.

Part Two

Marian Mediation in the Mission of the Church

∽◦⟨○⟩◦∼

IN THE MYSTERY of the Incarnation, the Son, the second person of the Trinity, became flesh. In the paschal mystery of his death, resurrection and ascension into heaven, Jesus, the God-man, accomplished God's ultimate victory of life over death and grace over sin.

At Pentecost, the Holy Spirit descended upon the body of Christ, the Church. The mission of the Church continues. At the Second Vatican Council, the Blessed Virgin Mary was proclaimed "Mother of the Church." This section will include a citation of the biblical texts used for the Marian feasts, a brief historical note concerning each feast, and reflections on the significance of the feast from various Catholic sources. Each section will conclude with reflection questions.

∽◦⟨○⟩◦∼

Solemnity of the Blessed Virgin Mary, the Mother of God

Readings

Numbers 6:22–27; Galatians 4:4–7; Luke 2:16–21

Historical Note

A feast in honor of Mary's maternity can be traced back to fifth-century Jerusalem. In A.D. 431 in Ephesus, the third ecumenical council of the Church declared that Mary was the Mother of God. The doctrine was an important development in understanding the true identity of Jesus. Mary is called *Theotokos* (God-bearer) because she is the mother of Jesus who is both God and man.

St. John of Damascus (c. 650–c. 750), a theologian and Doctor of the Church, grew up in Damascus, Syria, where he became familiar with the Islamic religion and its rulers. In the early eighth century, he entered

the monastic community of St. Sabas near Jerusalem, where he devoted his life to prayer, study, and writing. His writings on the Blessed Virgin Mary include four homilies (three of which are on the Assumption of Mary), and a strong defense of her divine maternity in On the Orthodox Faith (De Fide Orthodoxa). *His feast day is celebrated on December 4.*

Moreover we proclaim the holy Virgin to be in strict truth the Mother of God. For inasmuch as He who was born of her was true God, she who bore the true God incarnate is the true mother of God. For we hold that God was born of her, not implying that the divinity of the Word received from her the beginning of its being, but meaning that God the Word Himself, Who was begotten of the Father timelessly before the ages, and was with the Father and the Spirit without beginning and through eternity, took up His abode in these last days for the sake of our salvation in the Virgin's womb, and was without change made flesh and born of her. For the holy did not bear mere man but true God: and not mere God but God incarnate, Who did not bring down His body from Heaven, nor simply passed through the Virgin as channel, but received from her flesh of like essence to our own and subsisting in Himself. For if the body had come down from heaven and had not partaken of our nature, what would have been the use of His becoming man? For the purpose of God the Word becoming man was that the very same nature, which had sinned and fallen and become corrupted, should triumph over the deceiving tyrant and so be freed from corruption, just as the divine apostle puts it, *for since by man came death, by man came also the resurrection of the dead* [1 Cor 15:21].

Hence it is with justice and truth that we call the holy Mary the Mother of God. For this name embraces the whole mystery of the dispensation. For if she who bore Him is the Mother of God, assuredly He Who was born of her is God and likewise also man....

But we never say that the holy Virgin is the Mother of Christ.... For the Word Himself became flesh, having been in truth conceived of the Virgin, but coming forth as God with the assumed nature which, as soon as He was brought forth into being, was deified by Him, so that these three things took place simultaneously, the assumption of our nature, the coming into being, and the deification of the assumed nature by the Word. And thus it is that the holy Virgin is thought of and spoken of as the Mother of God, not only because of the nature of the Word, but also because of the deification of man's nature, the miracles of conception and of existence being wrought together, to wit, the conception of the Word, and the existence of the flesh in the Word Himself. For the very Mother of God in some marvelous manner was the means of fashioning the Framer of all things and of bestowing manhood on the God and Creator of all, Who deified the nature that He assumed, while the union preserved those things that were united just as they were united, that is to say, not only the divine nature of Christ but also His human nature, not only that which is above us but that which is of us.

St. John of Damascus, *On the Orthodox Faith* III, XII, in *The Nicene and Post-Nicene Fathers of the Christian Church*, second series, ed. Philip Schaff, DD, LLD, and Henry Wace, DD, vol. IX (Grand Rapids, MI: Eerdmans, 1983), 55–57.

Pope Paul VI, noting the celebration of this feast within the Octave of Christmas when we celebrate the birth of Jesus, the Prince of Peace, established January 1 as the World Day for Peace. In his 1974 apostolic exhortation Marialis Cultus (For the Right Ordering and Development of Devotion to the Blessed Virgin Mary), *the Pope wrote:*

In the revised ordering of the Christmas period it seems to us that the attention of all should be directed toward the restored Solemnity of Mary the holy Mother of God. This celebration, placed on January 1 in conformity with the ancient indication of the liturgy of the city of Rome, is meant to commemorate the part played by Mary in this mystery of salvation. It is meant also to exalt the singular dignity which this mystery brings to the "holy Mother ... through whom we were found worthy to receive the Author of life." It is likewise a fitting occasion for renewing adoration of the newborn Prince of Peace, for listening once more to the glad tidings of the angels (cf. Lk 2:14), and for imploring from God, through the Queen of Peace, the supreme gift of peace. It is for this reason that, in the happy concurrence of the Octave of Christmas and the first day of the year, we have instituted the World Day of Peace, an occasion that is gaining increasing support and already bringing forth fruits of peace in the hearts of many.

Pope Paul VI, *Marialis Cultus*
(Boston, MA: Daughters of St. Paul, 1974), no. 5.

Pope John Paul II had a deep appreciation for the mystery of Mary within the mystery of Christ and of the Church. In his 1987 encyclical Redemptoris Mater, *he highlighted the importance of this relationship.*

If it is true, as the Council itself proclaims, that "only in the mystery of the Incarnate Word does the mystery of man take on light," then this principle must be applied in a very particular way to that exceptional "daughter of the human race," that extraordinary "woman" who became the Mother of Christ. Only *in the mystery of Christ* is *her mystery fully made clear.* Thus has the Church sought to interpret it from the very beginning: the mystery of the Incarnation has enabled her to penetrate and to make ever clearer the mystery of the Mother of the Incarnate Word. The Council of Ephesus (431) was of decisive importance in clarifying this, for during that Council, to the great joy of Christians, the truth of the divine motherhood of Mary was solemnly confirmed as a truth of the Church's faith. Mary *is the Mother of God (= Theotokos)*, since by the power of the Holy Spirit she conceived in her virginal womb and brought into the world Jesus Christ, the Son of God, who is of one being with the Father.... Thus, through the mystery of Christ, on the horizon of the Church's faith there shines in its fullness the mystery of his Mother. In turn, the dogma of the divine motherhood of Mary was for the Council of Ephesus and is for the Church like a seal upon the dogma of the Incarnation, in which the Word truly assumes human nature into the unity of his person, without cancelling out that nature.

Pope John Paul II, *Redemptoris Mater*, no. 4.

Reflection Questions

❖ Mary is the Mother of God. Why is that of such critical importance in the Church's profession of her faith? How important is it to me?

❖ Do I fully appreciate the role of Mary in the mystery of Christ and the Church?

The Visitation (1519) by Raphael (Raffaello Sanzio) (1483–1520).
Museo del Prado, Madrid, Spain. Photo credit: Erich Lessing / Art Resource, NY.

Holy Family by Giulio Romano, (1499–1546). Galleria Palatina, Palazzo Pitti, Florence, Italy. Photo credit: Finsiel / Alinari / Art Resource, NY.

Icon with the Madonna, Anonymous. Palazzo Ducale, Venice, Italy.
Photo credit: Cameraphoto Arte, Venice / Art Resource, NY.

Immaculate Conception by Federico Barocci (1526–1612). Galleria Nazionale delle Marche, Urbino, Italy. Photo credit: Scala / Art Resource, NY.

Feast of the Presentation of the Lord

Readings

Malachi 3:1–4; Hebrews 2:14–18; Luke 2:22–40

Historical Note

This feast originated in fourth-century Jerusalem. It later moved to Antioch and Constantinople, where it received the name of *Hypapante* (meeting), a reference to the encounter that occurs between Jesus and Simeon in the Gospel story that is read on this day. In the early Middle Ages, the practice of lighting candles was added to the liturgical celebration. The feast has been known by several names: *Hypapante*, Presentation of the Lord, Candlemas Day, and the Purification of the Blessed Virgin Mary. The 1969 reform of the liturgical calendar restored the title of the Presentation of the Lord. In 1997, Pope John Paul II established the annual celebration of World Day for Consecrated Life on February 2. In his message to establish this special day of prayer for women and men who serve the Church and the world in consecrated life, he pointed out how the presentation of Jesus in the temple was "an eloquent icon of the total offering of one's life," and, therefore, presented a wonderful occasion to pray for all those who have made such an offering of their lives.

The Spanish pilgrim, Egeria, recorded the liturgy of the Feast of the Presentation of the Lord in Jerusalem between 381 and 388. She describes the celebration in these words:

The fortieth day after Epiphany is indeed celebrated here with the greatest solemnity. On that day there is a procession into the Anastasis, and all assemble there for the liturgy, and everything is performed in the prescribed manner with the greatest solemnity, just as on Easter Sunday. All the priests give sermons, and the bishop, too; and all preach on the Gospel text describing how on the fortieth day Joseph and Mary took the Lord to the temple, and how Simeon and Anna the prophetess, the daughter of Phanuel, saw Him, and what words they spoke on seeing the Lord, and of the offering which His parents brought. Afterwards, when all ceremonies have been performed in the prescribed manner, the Eucharist is then celebrated and the dismissal given.

Egeria: Diary of a Pilgrimage, trans. George F. Gingras, Ancient Christian Writers series, no. 38 (Ramsey, NJ: Paulist Press, 1970), 96–97.

Christopher O'Donnell, O.Carm. (1936–), is a Carmelite friar of the Irish Province, a theologian, and a prolific author of books and articles on theology, spirituality, and ecclesiology. He is senior lecturer in systematic theology at the Pontifical Milltown Institute in Dublin, Ireland. In 2006, Father O'Donnell received the Cardinal J. Wright Mariological Award, an award named after Cardinal John Wright, who served as episcopal chairman of the Mariological Society of America from 1951 to 1979. The award recognizes outstanding theological scholarship in the field of Marian studies. In this reflection, Father O'Donnell points out that the Orthodox Churches also celebrate the feast, which can enhance our appreciation for the core of Eastern spirituality. He writes:

At the heart of Eastern spirituality is the glory of the incarnation, the immense condescension of the divine majesty that allows the creator of the world to be the crucified one in order that divine life might erupt into the world. Glory and beauty surround his whole visible life, and especially his passion, death and resurrection....

Mary's role in the life of the Christian East is summed up in the tradition of icons. Mary appears in a privileged place on the iconastasis, the screen in front of the altar which depicts Christ, the angels, the patriarchs and saints. She is at the heart of the Communion of Saints: in the liturgy which unites heaven and earth she is present to the Church. There are several icon traditions of particular importance: firstly, there is the *Theotokos*, an icon of majesty with Mary dressed in subdued purple, whilst her Son is in royal gold; secondly, we have the *Deesis* (Mary in supplication), with the Virgin's hands upraised in intercession; thirdly, there is the *Hodegetria* (pointing the way) in which Mary holds the child Jesus in one arm and points to him with her other hand; fourthly, we note the *Eleousa* (the Mother of Tenderness), familiar especially in the St. Vladimir icon which shows Mary's eyes as seeming to look forward to the passion whilst she holds the child to her cheek.

Christopher O'Donnell, O.Carm., *At Worship with Mary: A Pastoral and Theological Study* (Wilmington, DE: Michael Glazier, 1988), 33, 35.

Reflection Questions

- ❖ Do I make an effort to promote consecrated life as a serious option for young people who are searching for a purposeful life in conformity with God's will?
- ❖ Do I promote consecrated life through my prayer, in family conversations, in my home parish, by inviting young people to visit a religious community?
- ❖ Do I pray to the Blessed Mother for men and women in consecrated life?
- ❖ How familiar am I with the richness of the spiritual traditions of Eastern spirituality?

Feast of Our Lady of Lourdes

Readings

No readings are assigned to this feast. The readings may come from the lectionary cycle for Ordinary Time, or from the Common of Masses of the Blessed Virgin Mary.

Historical Note

In 1858, Lourdes was a small village located in southern France in the foothills of the Pyrenees. Its population was about four thousand. Between February 11, 1858, and July 16, 1858, Bernadette Soubirous, a fourteen-year-old local girl from a poor family, experienced eighteen apparitions of the Blessed Virgin Mary at the cave or grotto of Massabielle. When Bernadette asked the Blessed Mother to identify herself, Mary said, "I am the Immaculate Conception." The dogma of Mary's Immaculate Conception had been solemnly defined in 1854.

Pilgrimages to Lourdes began around 1860. Some came seeking physical cures at the baths constructed at the spring of water Bernadette had used at the instructions of the Virgin Mary. In 1866, Bernadette joined the convent of the

Sisters of Charity of Nevers, where she died in 1879. She was canonized on December 8, 1933. The award-winning movie, *Song of Bernadette*, was produced in 1943. In the midst of the violence and chaos of World War II, it stimulated further interest in the story of Bernadette and in devotion to Our Lady of Lourdes.

Over the years, especially in light of the two world wars fought in Europe, pilgrims have streamed to the shrine at Lourdes. The complex includes a basilica in honor of the Blessed Mother under the title of the Immaculate Conception, a hospital and a Medical Observation Bureau, and the large underground Basilica of St. Pius X. That Pope had established the liturgical feast of Our Lady of Lourdes. Besides daily Mass at the site of the apparitions, the shrine holds a procession with the Blessed Sacrament led by the sick, and a torchlight Marian procession. Thousands of volunteers come from all over the world to assist those who wish to enter the baths.

Today, approximately 6 million pilgrims visit Lourdes each year. The year 2008 marks the 150th anniversary of the first apparition of the Blessed Virgin Mary to St. Bernadette.

Pope John Paul II visited the shrine twice: on August 15, 1983, and on August 14–15, 2004. In 1992, he established February 11 as World Day of the Sick. In 2004, on the occasion of the 150th anniversary of the proclamation of the dogma of the Immaculate Conception, a physically feeble Pope stayed with the sick at the Accueil Notre-Dame. In fact, this

would be his final international trip. An "accueil" is a reception area or a place that offers nursing accommodations for sick pilgrims. From the terrace of the Accueil Notre-Dame, John Paul II watched the evening torchlight procession and gave one of his reflections. He also concluded the Rosary procession at the Grotto of Massabielle, the place where the apparitions occurred, with this prayer:

Hail Mary,
poor and humble Woman,
Blessed by the Most High!
Virgin of hope,
dawn of a new era,
we join in your song of praise,
to celebrate the Lord's mercy,
to proclaim the coming of
the Kingdom
and the full liberation
of humanity.

Hail Mary,
lowly handmaid of the Lord,
Glorious Mother of Christ!
Faithful Virgin,
holy dwelling place of the Word,
Teach us to persevere
in listening
to the Word,
and to be docile
to the voice of the Spirit,
attentive to his promptings in the
depths of our conscience

and to his manifestations in the
events of history.

Hail Mary, Woman of Sorrows,
Mother of the living!
Virgin spouse beneath the Cross,
the new Eve,
Be our guide along the paths of
the world.
Teach us to experience and to
spread the love of Christ,
to stand with you before
the innumerable crosses
on which your Son
is still crucified.

Hail Mary, Woman of faith,
First of the disciples!
Virgin Mother of the Church,
help us always
to account for the hope
that is in us,
with trust in human goodness
and the Father's love.
Teach us to build up the world
beginning from within:
In the depths of silence
and prayer,
in the joy of fraternal love,
in the unique fruitfulness
of the Cross.

Holy Mary, Mother of believers,
Our Lady of Lourdes,
pray for us.
Amen.

Pope John Paul II, *L'Osservatore Romano*.
English edition, no. 34, August 25, 2004, p. 6.

Reflection Questions

❖ Do I understand the nature of my life as that of being on a pilgrimage—a journey toward heaven?

❖ The only meaning in suffering comes from its loving, redemptive quality. How do I understand the meaning of suffering?

❖ Do I pray for the sick? Do I visit the sick and take care of the sick, especially family members?

Solemnity of the Annunciation of the Lord

Readings

Isaiah 7:10–14; Hebrews 10: 4–10; Luke 1:26–38

Historical Note

The celebration of a feast of the Annunciation on March 25 probably dates to the seventh century, even though earlier sermons and a liturgical feast in late Advent clearly make up the history of this feast. Pope Paul VI noted its dual character when he wrote that "the feast was and is a joint one of Christ and of the Blessed Virgin: of the Word ... and of the Virgin, who becomes Mother of God" (*Marialis Cultus,* no. 6). He commented on how the liturgies of both the East and the West recognize in this feast a dual *fiat.* There is the *fiat* of the Incarnate Word, who enters human history, and the *fiat* of Mary, "the new Eve," the obedient virgin. Through her free consent and the working of the Holy Spirit, she "became the true Ark of the Covenant and the true Temple of God" (*MC,* no. 6). At the heart of this feast is the mystery of the Incar-nation. God enters the drama of human history, in a particular place and at a particular time, through and with the permission of the young Virgin of Nazareth. He enters human history and assumes the human condition in everything but sin! All pilgrims who travel to the Basilica of the Annunciation in Nazareth are struck by the inscription on the altar in the grotto where the angel Gabriel met the Virgin Mary: *Hic Verbum Caro factum est (Here the Word became flesh).*

The Akathistos Hymn celebrates the Marian doctrine and piety of the Churches of the Byzantine Rite. The word Akathistos / a-kathistos *in Greek means "not-seated," because it is to be sung or recited "standing." There has been debate over its precise origins. Written over a period of time between the fifth and seventh centuries, it is celebrated on the fifth Saturday of Lent, called "Saturday of the Akathistos." This date in the liturgical calendar locates it close to the solemnity of the Annunciation. The content of the hymn links the mystery of Christmas to the paschal mystery. We move from Mary's presence at the birth of Jesus to her presence at our rebirth in the sacramental waters of baptism. On December 8, 2000, Pope John Paul II met with representatives of other Byzantine Catholic Churches in the Basilica of St. Mary Major in Rome. Gathered before the icon of the Salus Populi Romani, they included the Akathistos Hymn in their prayer. The Pope had expressed his desire on other occasions that the hymn be used, and he himself presided over such times of prayer. In 1981, for example, he used it to commemorate the anniversaries of the First Council of Constantinople (381) and the Council of Ephesus (431). The* Akathistos *Hymn was sung in Greek, Old Slavonic, Arabic, and other languages used by the Churches of the Byzantine Rite. The stanzas sing of the infancy narratives of the Gospel and the place of Mary, the* Theotokos, *in the mystery of Christ and in the teaching of the Church. Each stanza concludes with the phrase,*

"Rejoice or Hail, Thou Bride Unwedded!" Here the second stanza offers a glimpse into the beauty of this profound, prayerful song of contemplation and praise. The terms kontakion/ekos/oikoi *refer to the stanzas.*

KONTAKION 2

Seeing herself to be chaste, the holy one said boldly to Gabriel: The marvel of thy speech is difficult for my soul to accept. How canst thou speak of a birth from a seedless conception? And She cried: Alleluia!

EKOS 2

Seeking to know knowledge that cannot be known, the Virgin cried to the ministering one: Tell me, how can a son be born from a chaste womb? Then he spake to Her in fear, only crying aloud thus:

Rejoice, initiate of God's ineffable will: Rejoice,
    assurance of those who pray in silence!

Rejoice, beginning of Christ's miracles: Rejoice,
    crown of His dogmas!

Rejoice, heavenly ladder by which God came down: Rejoice,
    bridge that conveyest us from earth to Heaven!

Rejoice, wonder of angels sounded abroad: Rejoice,
    wound of demons bewailed afar!

Rejoice, Thou who ineffably gavest birth to the Light:
    Rejoice, Thou who didst reveal Thy secret to
    none!

Rejoice, Thou who surpassest the knowledge of the
   wise: Rejoice, Thou who givest light to the minds of
   the faithful!
Rejoice, Thou Bride Unwedded!

Book of Akathists
(Jordanville, NY: Holy Trinity Monastery, 1994), 122.

*Catherine de Hueck Doherty (1896–1985) was born in Russia on
August 15, 1896. She was raised in the Russian Orthodox Church. At
the age of fifteen, she married her cousin, Baron Boris de Hueck. The
young couple left Russia during the Bolshevik Revolution, and after set-
tling in England, she was received into the Catholic Church.*

*In 1921, Catherine and Boris went to Toronto. She became a popu-
lar lecturer throughout the United States. In 1930, she experienced an
intellectual and spiritual conversion that created within her the desire to
live the Gospel message of radical poverty in the context of an evangelical community lifestyle. She met and developed a close friendship with
Dorothy Day, both of whom promoted the social justice teaching of the
Church. To minister to the poor in Toronto, Catherine opened
Friendship House. At the suggestion of Father John LaFarge, SJ, the
Jesuit social gospel activist, she opened another Friendship House in
Harlem, New York, in 1938. Thomas Merton was among those who
volunteered to serve at the Harlem Friendship House. Catherine's mar-
riage to Boris ended and was eventually declared null by the Catholic
Church. In 1943, she married Eddie Doherty. In 1947, following her
resignation as director general of the Friendship House in Harlem,
Catherine and Eddie moved to Combermere, Ontario, Canada.*

*Catherine was deeply committed to the role of the laity in the promo-
tion of the Gospel. In 1951, she attended the first lay congress in Rome,*

Italy. In that same year, she and Eddie made an act of consecration to Jesus through Mary according to the method of St. Louis de Montfort. Three years later, the community of Madonna House was established at Combermere. Based on the evangelical counsels of poverty, chastity, and obedience, it was placed under the patronage of Mary, Mother of the Church. Catherine died on December 14, 1985. The bishop of Pembroke has opened the cause for her canonization.

Catherine's writings introduced the influence of her Russian spirituality into her critique of Western culture. Perhaps the two most popular terms associated with her works are: poustinia, *the Russian term for "a desertlike solitude," and* sobornost, *the Russian word for "communion of mind and heart with the Blessed Trinity." Catherine believed that the Western world needs to value solitude as a place to meet God. Against the rampant individualism of the age, the West also needs genuine communion of mind and heart as an expression of the Trinitarian imprint that lies within us.*

Linda Lambeth, in the foreword to Bogoroditza: She Who Gave Birth to God, *writes that Catherine had a great desire to write a book on Mary. However, she died before such a task could be completed. In* Bogoroditza, *Lambeth has compiled a collection of Catherine Doherty's reflections on the important role Mary plays in our lives. These excerpts are from her talk entitled "Fiat," given to laity and clergy on the occasion of the renewal of their commitment to the spirit of Madonna House.*

Mary and the apostolate are enclosed in a little word—*fiat.* Think of it. If you consider this one little word, you will understand its immensity. You will know that all that we are trying to teach you, and all that is being taught to us all, can be encompassed in this *fiat,* for the only reason for a *fiat* is caritas—love. And the fruit of *fiat* and *caritas* is *pax*—peace.

Mary and the apostolate. So simple, so clear, so easy to understand. When you really get down to hard brass tacks, you can throw out all your books if you know how to love.

She and our apostolate are one. She became the mother of the apostolate the moment she pronounced the word *fiat*, and a blinding light that even the angel could not look upon descended upon her and the Holy Spirit overshadowed her and she conceived the Son of God.

In another way, the same happens to each one of us. The Holy Spirit overshadows us with his graces, and with his help we each shall die to self, and have an Advent, a time of waiting, of spiritual pregnancy with Christ.

Each of us exists, even as Mary did, to give birth to Christ in us. She was full of grace. We will be full of grace too. (Not in the manner that she was, without stain of original sin; nevertheless, we will be.) She will help us to die to self, so that when we, who began our apostolate with a *fiat*, die and finish our apostolate, we will be able to say with the ringing voice of St. Paul, "I live not, Christ lives in me." ...

You will find your Bethlehem, each one of you. There will come a day in your life when you really will give birth to Christ, in the stable of Arizona, in the desert of Africa, in the snows of Canada, wherever your visitation will lead you. There, you shall give birth to Christ for all to see....

Mary will be there. She is always there at the birth of her Son in people's hearts. She is the midwife and the mother of this delicate and beautiful meeting of her Spouse, the Holy Spirit, and a human soul.

Then you will know the hidden years of Nazareth within your soul. You will know them blending together, covering time and space, because these things do not historically or even poetically follow one after another. The spiritual life is a mixture of all things at once: the joyful, the sorrowful, and the glorious mysteries. So you will know the whole life of a woman with two men, Jesus and Joseph, and in Jesus, with God.

And so you weave a sort of pattern out of your life, now going to Bethlehem, now to Nazareth. Mary will lead you to the little village of Nazareth and it will be a hidden village. She has the keys to all doors in heaven and on earth, and she will open the path for you and take you in.

Mary will take you into a house where she dwelt for thirty years with God and Joseph. And you will dwell in that house likewise. It will be a hidden house. People will not understand whom you represent and why you are there. There will be need for flights to Egypt; there will be persecution; there will be lies told about you.

Suddenly, one day, you will find yourself side-by-side with Mary in the passion of Christ; next you will return just as suddenly to Nazareth. For we are weak and small, and Our Lady gently shows us the secrets that we must know so as to reach her Son and become one with him.

We can put all this another way. The relationship between Mary and the apostolate is very simple. It's a school of love, where the Mother of Fair Love will teach you, and when you are in doubt, will comfort you. And when you are in the dark night of the soul, she will sing her lullabies to you. And across the darkness when all is aridity, when her Son seems to have disappeared, her soft voice will suddenly come to you. Who knows, will she sing in Aramaic, in Hebrew, or in your own tongue? It matters not. Her voice is like oil on a wounded heart. No matter how dark the night, there will be light, because Mary will be there.

Catherine de Hueck Doherty, *Bogoroditza: She Who Gave Birth to God*, comp. Linda Lambeth (Combermere, Ontario: Madonna House Publications, 1998), 106, 107, 108, 109.

James Cardinal Hickey (1920–2004) was born in Midland, Michigan, in 1920. In 1946, he was ordained a priest for the Diocese of Saginaw, Michigan, where he served as a pastor, vocations director, and rector. In 1967, he was ordained an auxiliary bishop for Saginaw. He served as rector of the Pontifical North American College from 1969 to 1974, when he was appointed Bishop of the Diocese of Cleveland, Ohio. From 1980 until 2000, he served as Archbishop of the Archdiocese of Washington. In 1988, Pope John Paul II named him to the College of Cardinals. Throughout his life, Cardinal Hickey was known for his gentle spirit, commitment to Catholic education, the promotion of vocations, and an evangelical zeal for the poor.

In 1988, John Paul II invited him to preach the annual Lenten retreat for the papal household, for which Cardinal Hickey chose the theme "Mary at the Foot of the Cross." In the excerpts from this conference, he reflected on the meaning of the annunciation in the life of the Blessed Virgin.

The dialogue with the Angel ends abruptly. "And Mary said, 'Behold, I am the handmaid of the Lord; let it be to me according to your word.' And the Angel departed from her" (Lk 1:38). We too have shared Mary's wonderment and even her distress at her encounter with the Angel. The Angel departed without giving her a detailed set of instructions replete with fallback plans. The Angel left her! Yet Mary knew that God's wisdom had entrusted her with a mission to which she had assented. She also knew that her once-for-all assent would call for ratification again and again as the mysterious plan of God unfolded.

The obedience that Mary manifested at the Annunciation was absolute. It was trusting. At the same time, however, her absolute, trusting obedience was clearly more than a prompt response to a series of minute commands. In fact, these were lacking. There was no need for them, for we find in Mary a heart that was truly attuned to the ways of God. Mary, whose vision was unclouded by sin, loved the Law and the prophets. They were her delight. Through them, she was rendered present to God, totally available for whatever he wanted. She was deeply familiar with all the Lord was revealing about himself, and she accepted everything he revealed with great faith. She experienced a great *consonance* with God and the ways of God; it was more than a feeling—rather, a deep union of her whole person with the very counsels of God.

From the beginning of her life, the Word of God was present to Mary, and Mary was present to the Word. In her the Word became flesh. In her home, the Word-made-flesh dwelt. Her life was at the disposal of the Word.

James Cardinal Hickey, *Mary at the Foot of the Cross*
(San Francisco: Ignatius Press, 1988), 81–82.

Reflection Questions

❖ Do I recognize the messengers God sends to me to obtain my permission so that he can work through me?

❖ What means do I use to cultivate an interior disposition of the heart that will make me completely open and desirous of doing God's will?

❖ How do I cultivate the virtue of obedience? Do I appreciate obedience to God and the Church as a sign of spiritual, emotional maturity?

MAY 31

Feast of the Visitation of the Blessed Virgin Mary

Readings

Zephaniah 3:14–18 or Romans 12:9–16b; Luke 1:39–56

Historical Note

At the time of the Western Schism (1378–1417), the Church suffered from the pain of division from within. This context provides the background for the introduction of the feast of the Visitation. An antipope named Clement VII was in Avignon, and Pope Urban VI was in Rome. On June 16, 1386, the Archbishop of Prague, John Jenstein, promulgated the introduction of the feast during a diocesan synod. The synod hoped that this new Marian feast would also restore unity to a fractured Church. Pope Urban VI wanted to extend the feast throughout the Western Church, but because of the schism, only those churches in communion with Rome celebrated the feast. In 1441, at the Council of Basle, a proper Mass with a feast on July 2 was established for the Western Church. The date was moved to May 31 in the liturgical reform of 1969.

Carlo Carretto (1910–1988) was born in northern Italy. He devoted much of his young life to teaching and active involvement with a lay apostolate that was coordinated by "Catholic Action." In 1945, at the request of Pope Pius XII, Carretto organized the National Association of Catholic Teachers. From 1946 until 1952, he also served as president of the Italian Youth of Catholic Action.

He then decided to join the religious community of the Little Brothers of Jesus. This group, founded by Charles de Foucauld (1858–1916), whom Pope Benedict XVI beatified in 2005, was dedicated to a life of poverty and prayer in the spirit of the hidden life of Nazareth. Carlo Carretto entered the community in El Abiodh, Algeria, in the Sahara desert. For ten years, he lived the life of a hermit, having profound experiences of prayer, which he captured in his Letters from the Desert. *In 1964, he returned to Italy, where he gained a reputation as a leading spiritual writer and retreat director. A man with great devotion to St. Francis of Assisi, Carretto died on October 4, 1988 (the feast of St. Francis). In this reflection from his work* Blessed Are You Who Believed, *Carretto's prayer is structured around his request that the Blessed Mother share with him her experience of her visit to Elizabeth.*

Oh the joy I [Mary] felt when he [God] told me this! But what terror and darkness I had been through.

I came to understand that this is the very nature of faith and that we have to get used to living in darkness.

And something else happened which helped to alleviate my distress in those months.

You [Carlo C.] know that the angel had given me a sign to support me in my weakness. He told me that my cousin Elizabeth was in the sixth month of an amazing pregnancy —amazing, because all of us in the family knew her to be barren.

It was decided that I should go and visit her in Ain-Karim in Judea where she lived.

I didn't have to be persuaded to leave!

It was my mother's idea because she was worried about the neighbours seeing me big with child, and she didn't want any gossip.

I left at night and I was really pleased to be getting away from Nazareth where there were so many inquisitive eyes and I couldn't tell everyone the facts of the situation.

I found my cousin already near her time, and very happy. She had longed for a child.

The Lord must have explained things to her too, because when I arrived she seemed to know everything, everything, everything.

She started to sing for joy, and I sang with her.

We must both have seemed mad, but mad with love.

And there was a third being who seemed to be mad with joy.

This was someone very small, the future John, who leapt in Elizabeth's womb as if to welcome Jesus who was in mine.

I shall never forget those days.

But Elizabeth, who knew all about faith, dark faith, and who had suffered so much in her life, said something to me which pleased me very much and seemed like a reward for all my loneliness in those months. She said:

"Blessed are you who believed" (Lk 1:44).

And she repeated it every time she saw me and touched my belly, touched it as if to touch Jesus, the new Moses who was to come into the world.

Carlo Carretto, *Blessed Are You Who Believed*, trans. Barbara Well.
(Maryknoll, NY: Orbis, 1982), 11–12.

Romano Guardini (1885–1968) was born in northern Italy but lived in Germany. In his youth, his intellectual curiosity engaged him in the studies of chemistry and economics. In 1905, after a profound crisis of faith, Guardini turned to the study of theology. He was ordained a priest in 1910. From 1922 until the Nazis expelled him in 1939, Guardini taught philosophy and the Christian vision of life at the University of Berlin. From 1948 to 1963, he taught at the University of Tübingen. His major life experiences had an enormous impact on his writing: two world wars in Germany, the growth of a nihilistic existentialism, Nazism, and his involvement with the Catholic Youth Movement.

His writing expressed the hope he found in the importance of a personal relationship with Jesus Christ as Lord, in the cultivation of a strong prayer life, and in genuine participation in the sacred liturgy of the Church. His work The Rosary of Our Lady *offers a simple yet profound reflection on what one does when one prays the Rosary. He also offers a rich meditation on the various mysteries of the Rosary. Here that meditation is on the Second Joyful Mystery, the Visitation.*

This is the time after the angel's Annunciation that was, for Mary, at once happy and distressing. No woman has ever borne such gladness within her. But neither was any woman ever imprisoned in such silence. For how could she speak of the event so that the listener would believe her? Not even he to whom she was espoused for life understood until an angel enlightened him in a dream.

Here began the serious part of resignation. For honor or dishonor, for life and death, she was in God's hands. She left her home, and crossed the mountains to Elizabeth, that motherly woman to whom she was connected by old ties of trust. She, who was often afflicted, would know what had happened. And she did know, for the spirit that had worked the mystery in Mary also filled Elizabeth, so that she knew the truth before Mary said a word: "Blessed are thou among women and blessed is the fruit of thy womb!" The whole mystery is filled with the unspeakable intimacy in which Mary carried the life of the God-man, giving Him hers and receiving of His.

In every Christian life there is a sacred domain of nascent growth in which dwells Christ—a domain in which we are more firmly rooted than we are in our own. There He works and grows, takes possession of our being, draws our strength toward Himself, penetrates our thoughts and volition, and sways our emotions and sentiments, so that the word of the Apostle comes true: "It is now no longer I that live, but Christ lives in me" (Gal 2:20).

Romano Guardini, *The Rosary of Our Lady*, trans. H. von Schuecking. (Manchester, NH: Sophia Institute Press, 1994), 87–88.

Adrienne von Speyr in Handmaid of the Lord *sees the Magnificat as confirmation of Mary's absorption of the Word, and her mission to mediate the work of her Son:*

The Magnificat is an expression of the degree to which the Mother treasures all the words of God in her heart. She says what she is enjoined to say; about the rest she is silent. But from her words one senses how much more she knows. Her silence is, not forgetful, but re-collecting. She takes everything up into her prayer. And now that the Son is within her, her prayer is more than ever inseparable from the prayer of her Son. She *is* the meditation of her Son. Her prayer belongs to the Son and cannot be separated from his. Their prayer flows together, just as they are physically one at this moment. And although, humanly speaking, it is perhaps the Mother who forms the words and directs the thoughts since the Son cannot yet bring to his lips a human prayer, the content of the prayer is nevertheless determined and filled by the Son. He gives life to her thoughts and words. Thus, she is perfect contemplation because the Son has been wholly taken up into her and he forms her meditation completely according to his law and will.

The time of pregnancy is for Mary a time of perfect contemplation, of exhaustive listening to the Son. But at the same time it is a time of action, for she goes to Elizabeth to bring her the Son, to pass on the gift she has received from God. She does this not only by giving him to others as she feels him within her physically, but also by praying the Magnificat as part of her mission. For this too is the Son's presence in her, and all the words she speaks in her mission are an expression of the divine Word within her. And while Elizabeth hears these words, she is already praying along with them so that Mary, commissioned by her Son, is already working apostolically and teaching men to pray. In carrying the Lord to others physically and spiritually, she is doing what the Church will do later when she brings men the Eucharist. The Lord whom the Mother bears and the Lord in the Host are the same, and this one Lord has only one thought: to give himself away, to share his very substance, in an infinite manner. The Mother understood this from the beginning and never bore anything in mind except giving the Son to the world.

Adrienne von Speyr, *Handmaid of the Lord*, 52–53.

Venerable John Henry Cardinal Newman (1801–1890) was born in London, ordained an Anglican priest, and became a Catholic in 1845. Newman entered the oratory that St. Philip Neri had founded in the sixteenth century, and brought it to England. In 1879, Pope Leo XIII named Newman to the College of Cardinals. In 1991, Pope John Paul II declared him "venerable" as the cause of his canonization advanced.

Cardinal wrote many volumes. His thoughts on the role of the Blessed Virgin Mary can be found in several works, including sermons; his Letter to E .B. Pusey, *the Anglican theologian; and in his comments on Catholic devotions. Newman's work* On Consulting the Faithful in Matters of Doctrine *(1859) considers the process that Blessed Pope Pius IX followed in defining the dogma of the Immaculate Conception (1854), which took account of the testimony of the faithful over the centuries. An excerpt from his reflection on the petition, "Mary Is the 'Domus Aurea,' House of Gold" of the Litany of Loreto follows.*

Why is she called a *House?* And why is she called *Golden?* Gold is the most beautiful, the most valuable, of all metals. Silver, copper, and steel may in their way be made good to the eye, but nothing is so rich, so splendid, as gold. We have few opportunities of seeing it in any quantity; but anyone who has seen a large number of bright gold coins knows how magnificent is the look of gold. Hence it is that in Scripture the Holy City is, by a figure of speech, called Golden. "The City," says St. John, "was pure gold, as it were transparent glass." He means of course to give us a notion of the wondrous beautifulness of heaven, by comparing it with what is the most beautiful of all the substances which we see on earth.

Therefore it is that Mary too is called *golden;* because her graces, her virtues, her innocence, her purity, are of that transcendent brilliancy and dazzling perfection, so costly, so exquisite, that the angels cannot, so to say, keep their eyes off her any more than we could help gazing upon any great work of gold.

But observe further, she is a *golden house*, or, I will rather say, a *golden palace*. Let us imagine we saw a whole palace or large church all made of gold, from the foundations to the roof; such, in regard to the number, the variety, the extent of her spiritual excellence, is Mary.

But why called a *house* or palace? And *whose* palace? She is the house and the palace of the Great King, of God Himself. Our Lord, the Co-equal Son of God, once dwelt in her. He was her Guest; nay, more than a guest, for a guest comes into a house as well as leaves it. But our Lord was actually *born* in this holy house. He took His flesh and His blood from this house, from the flesh, from the veins of Mary. Rightly then was she made to be of pure gold, because she was to give of that gold to form the body of the Son of God. She was *golden* in her conception, *golden* in her birth. She went through the fire of her suffering like gold in the furnace, and when she ascended on high, she was, in the words of our hymn,

> Above all the Angels in glory untold.
> Standing next to the King in a vesture of gold.

John Henry Newman, Prayers, Verses and Devotions
(San Francisco: Ignatius Press, 2000), 121–22.

Reflection Questions

❖ Am I aware that I too am a temple/an ark/a tabernacle called to bring Jesus to others?

❖ Do I seek the guidance of the Blessed Mother in knowing to whom, when, and in what way I should commit myself to some form of apostolic work?

❖ Mary was pregnant and carried Jesus over hills and difficult terrain to the village of Elizabeth. Do I seek Mary's protection on the pilgrimage of my life with its suffering and challenges?

❖ How do I understand contemplative prayer? Do I use the Rosary as a form of contemplative prayer?

Feast of the Immaculate Heart of Mary[*]

Readings

The first reading can follow the lectionary cycle for Ordinary Time, or it may be chosen from the Common of Masses of the Blessed Virgin Mary. The Gospel is proper, Luke 2:41–51.

Historical Notes

The following comes from the research of Father Danilo Sartor, OSM, who traces the origins of devotion to Mary's heart, in which she contemplated the mystery of Jesus, to the Patristic writers of East and West. They prayerfully commented on the two passages of St. Luke's Gospel that mention Mary's pondering in her heart: Luke 2:19, 51.

---

* This feast, an obligatory memorial, is celebrated on the day after the Solemnity of the Sacred Heart, or on the Saturday after the second Sunday after Pentecost.

The development of a Catholic spirituality and devotion to the heart of Mary continued in the Middle Ages in the works of St. Bernard of Clairvaux (1090–1153), the female mystics of Helfta, especially St. Gertrude the Great (1252–1302), and St. Bernardine of Siena (1380–1444). St. John Eudes (1601–1680) promoted devotion to the hearts of Jesus and Mary and the development of its liturgical cult. Through his theological treatises and through his preaching, the devotion became very popular among the faithful and was also expressed in art and in the consecration of churches and oratories.

The devotion has continued to grow following the spread of devotion to the Miraculous Medal (1830), and the apparitions of the Blessed Virgin Mary at Fatima (1917). In 1942, Pope Pius XII consecrated the world to the Immaculate Heart of Mary. Two years later, he extended the liturgical feast of the Immaculate Heart to the entire Church. On May 13, 1981, the anniversary of the first apparition of the Blessed Mother to the three children of Fatima, Pope John Paul II was shot in St. Peter's Square in Rome. He believed that it was through the intercession of Our Lady of Fatima that his life was spared. The following year, he traveled as a pilgrim to Fatima and placed the assassin's bullet in the crown worn by the statue of Our Lady of Fatima. On several occasions during his pontificate, he renewed the consecration of the world to the Immaculate Heart of Mary.

Sartor, *Nuovo Dizionario di Mariologia*, 446.

The role of the heart of Mary in God's plan of salvation appeared in Pope John Paul II's very first encyclical letter. In Redemptor Hominis *(Redeemer of Man), published on March 4, 1979, the Pope wrote:*

We can say that the mystery of the Redemption took shape beneath the heart of the Virgin of Nazareth when she pronounced her *"fiat."* From then on, under the special influence of the Holy Spirit, this heart, the heart of both a virgin and a mother, has always followed the work of her Son and has gone out to all those whom Christ has embraced and continues to embrace with inexhaustible love. For that reason her heart must also have the inexhaustibility of a mother.

Pope John Paul II, *Redemptor Hominis*
(Washington, DC: United States Catholic Conference, 1979), no. 22.

In his homily at Fatima in 1982, Pope John Paul II addressed the meaning of an act of consecration to the heart of Mary in these words:

On the Cross Christ said: "Woman, behold your Son!" With these words he opened in a new way his Mother's heart. A little later, the Roman soldier's spear pierced the side of the Crucified One. That pierced heart became a sign of the redemption achieved through the death of the Lamb of God.

The Immaculate Heart of Mary, opened with the words "Woman, behold your son!" is spiritually united with the heart of her Son opened by the soldier's spear. Mary's heart was opened by the same love for man and for the world with which Christ loved man and the world, offering himself for them on the Cross, until the soldier's spear struck that blow.

Consecrating the world to the Immaculate Heart of Mary means drawing near, through the Mother's intercession, to the very fountain of life that sprang from Golgotha. This Fountain pours forth unceasingly redemption and grace. In it reparation is made continually for the sins of the world. It is a ceaseless source of new life and holiness.

Consecrating the world to the Immaculate Heart of the Mother means returning beneath the Cross of the Son. It means consecrating this world to the pierced Heart of the Saviour, bringing it back to the very source of its Redemption. Redemption is always greater than man's sin and the "sin of the world." The power of the Redemption is infinitely superior to the whole range of evil in man and the world.

The Heart of the Mother is aware of this, more than any other heart in the whole universe, visible and invisible.

And so she calls us.

She not only calls us to be converted: she calls us to accept her motherly help to return to the source of Redemption.

Consecrating ourselves to Mary means accepting her help to offer ourselves and the whole of mankind to *Him who is Holy*, infinitely Holy; it means accepting her help—by having recourse to her motherly Heart, which beneath the Cross was opened to love for every human being, for the whole world—in order to offer the world, the individual human being, mankind as a whole, and all the nations to Him who is infinitely Holy. God's holiness showed itself in the redemption of man, of the world, of the whole of mankind, and of the nations: a redemption brought about through the sacrifice of the Cross. "For their sake *I consecrate myself,*" Jesus had said (Jn 17:19).

> Pope John Paul II, Homily at Mass in Fatima on May 13, 1982.
> *L'Osservatore Romano*. English edition, May 17, 1982, p. 3.

Reflection Questions

❖ How do I understand the act of consecration to the Immaculate Heart of Mary in light of Pope John Paul's reflection?

❖ Am I prepared to make a personal act of consecration to her Immaculate Heart?

Feast of Our Lady of Mount Carmel

Readings

No readings are assigned to this feast. The readings may come from the lectionary cycle for Ordinary Time, or from the Common of Masses of the Blessed Virgin Mary.

Historical Note

The late eleventh and early twelfth centuries saw an increased growth in the eremitical life. The early crusaders established the Latin Kingdom of Jerusalem. Hermits were attracted to Palestine at that time, and by the late twelfth century, a community had formed on the mountain range that runs alongside the Mediterranean Sea south of the present-day city of Haifa. Joachim Smet, O.Carm., writes that one group of hermits who lived on Mt. Carmel near "Elijah's Well" received a Rule that shaped their lifestyle as a community. It was written by St. Albert of Vercelli, the Latin Patriarch of Jerusalem, between 1206 and 1214. The small chapel in the midst of the cells of these hermits was dedicated to the Blessed Virgin Mary. The group became known as the "Brothers of Our Lady of Mount Carmel" (Smet, 8). The history of Carmelite spirituality includes friars, sisters, and those women and men who have adopted a Carmelite vision of the Gospel and adapted it to their particular state in life. This latter group, the Carmelite Third Order, was established in 1476. Christopher O'Donnell, O.Carm., a Catholic theologian and Carmelite friar, points to the ways in which theological reflection, liturgical practice, contemplative prayer, and devotional practices, for example, the wearing of the Brown Scapular, all highlight the common heritage shared by the members of the First, Second, and Third Orders in honoring Mary "as Patroness, Mother, Sister and Most Pure Virgin" (O'Donnell, *Carmel and Mary*, 84).The liturgical feast in honor of Our Lady of Mount Carmel was established for the universal Church in 1726.

Jessica Powers (1905–1988) from her earliest years in school cultivated a love of writing, poetry, and the desire for contemplation and prayer. From 1937 to 1941, Jessica lived in New York City in the home of the famous Thomistic philosopher, Anton Pegis, along with his wife and their children. This gave Jessica the opportunity to study, become associated with the Catholic literary revival, enter various reading and cultural circles, and discover her growing desire for a deeper life of prayer.

In 1941, she entered the Carmelite monastery of Mother of God, in Milwaukee, Wisconsin, where she took the name Sister Miriam of the Holy Spirit. There, immersed in a life of prayer and contemplation, Powers continued to write poetry until her death in 1988. In the poem

"The Cloud of Carmel," Powers gives expression to her own contemplation of the mystery of Mary in the Carmelite tradition.

THE CLOUD OF CARMEL

"The Lord promised that He would dwell in a cloud."
   — (2 Chronicles 6:1)

Symbol of star or lily of the snows,
rainbow or root or vine or fruit-filled tree:
these image the immaculate to me
less than a little cloud, a little light cloud rising
from Orient waters cleft by prophecy.
And as the Virgin in a most surprising
maternity bore God and our doomed race,
I who bear God in the mysteries of grace
beseech her: Cloud, encompass God and me.

Nothing defiled can touch the cloud of Mary.
God as a child willed to be safe in her,
and the Divine Indweller sets His throne
deep in a cloud in me, His sanctuary.
I pray, O wrap me, Cloud, ... light Cloud of Carmel
within whose purity my vows were sown
to lift their secrecies to God alone.
Say to my soul, the timorous and small
house of a Presence that it cannot see
and frightened acre of a Deity,
say in the fullness of your clemency:
I have enclosed you all.

You are in whiteness of a lighted lamb wool;
you are in softness of a summer wind lull.
O hut of God, deepen your faith anew.
Enfolded in this motherhood of mine,
all that is beautiful and all divine
is safe in you.

(1946)

Jessica Powers, "The Cloud of Carmel," in *The Selected Poetry of Jessica Powers*, ed. Regina Siegfried, ASC, and Robert Morneau (Washington, DC: ICS Publications, 1999), 56.

Reflection Questions

❖ Do I include the insights of some of the Carmelite authors/saints in my appreciation for the Virgin Mary's role in the spiritual life, for example, St. Teresa of Jesus, St. John of the Cross, St. Therese of the Child Jesus, St. Elizabeth of the Trinity, St. Teresa Benedicta of the Cross, Bl. Titus Brandsma, Sr. Jessica Powers?

❖ Have I considered joining a Third Order to find a spiritual family who will assist me to live a deeper spiritual life according to my state of life (married, widowed, single, divorced, diocesan priest, etc.)?

Feast of the Dedication of the Basilica of St. Mary Major

Readings

No readings are assigned to this feast. The readings may come from the lectionary cycle for Ordinary Time, or from the Common of Masses of the Blessed Virgin Mary.

Historical Note

Legend and the iconographic depiction found within the Basilica of St. Mary Major in Rome attribute the origin of this church to a fourth-century vision of the Blessed Mother. She asked that a church be constructed on the Esquiline hill where snow would fall on August 5! Following the Council of Ephesus (431), Pope Sixtus III ordered the construction of the church in honor of the conciliar proclamation of Mary as the Mother of God (*Theotokos*). The basilica contains a relic of the crib where Jesus was born and an icon of the Blessed Mother under the title *Salus Populi Romani* (Salvation of the Roman People). Over the centuries, the icon has been used on numerous occasions in processions and liturgical events within the church.

Joseph Cardinal Ratzinger (1927–), Pope Benedict XVI, was born at Marktl am Inn, Germany, on April 16, 1927. He was raised in a small village near the Austrian border, not far from Salzburg. Because of his strong family ties and good education in a Catholic milieu, he rejected the teachings of the Nazi regime, although he was drafted into military service. After the war, he studied theology, and on June 29, 1951, he was ordained a priest. In 1953, he obtained his doctorate in theology. From 1959 to 1969, he taught dogmatic and fundamental theology at many prestigious universities throughout Germany. He also served as the theological advisor ("expert") to Cardinal Joseph Frings, the Archbishop of Cologne, during the Second Vatican Council (1962–1965). In 1972, Ratzinger, Hans Urs von Balthasar, Henri de Lubac, and others established the theological journal Communio.*

In 1977, Pope Paul VI named him Archbishop of Munich and Freising, and on June 27 of the same year, elevated him to the College of Cardinals. Pope John Paul II appointed Cardinal Ratzinger to the position of Prefect of the Congregation of the Faith in 1981. Cardinal Ratzinger held this position until his election as pope on April 19, 2005.*

In the foreword to his book Images of Hope: Meditations on Major Feasts, *then Cardinal Ratzinger published a collection of his reflections on the liturgical year. A unique aspect of this work is the Cardinal's desire to present his reflections within the background of the artistic treasures found in the churches of Rome. His essay on the August 5 celebration of the dedication of the Basilica of St. Mary Major includes a reflection on the relic of the manger where Jesus was born, and the popular icon of Mary under the title of* Salus Populi Romani. *First, we read the Cardinal's reflection on the relic of the manger.*

... This church is a Christmas church....

The mosaics on both the long sides of the nave present, so to speak, all of history as the procession of mankind to the Redeemer. In the middle, above the arch of triumph, to which the aisles lead, where we would expect the birth of Christ to be represented, we find instead only an empty throne and on it a crown, a ruler's mantle, and the cross. On the footstool lies the bundle of history like a pillow bound together with seven red threads. The empty throne, the cross, and history at its feet—that is the Christmas image of this church, which claimed and claims to be the Bethlehem of Rome. Why? If we wish to understand the image we have first to recall that the arch of triumph stands above the crypt that originally was built as the replica of the cave of Bethlehem in which Christ came into the world. Here the relic was and is still venerated that according to tradition is the manger of Bethlehem. So here the procession of history, all the splendor of the mosaics, is abruptly pulled down into the cave, into the stable. The images fall down into reality. The throne is empty, for the Lord has come down into the stable. The central mosaic, to which everything leads, is likewise only the hand that is extended to us so that we might discover the leap from the images to reality. The rhythm of the space pulls us into a sudden change when it thrusts us out of the brilliant heights of ancient art in the mosaics directly into the depth of the cave, of the stable. It seeks to lead us into the transition from religious aestheticism to the act of faith....

It would remain a beautiful dream, a fleeting feeling without binding authority and, therefore, without power, if we did not let ourselves be taken to the next step, namely, to the Yes of faith. Then something further becomes clear: the cave is not empty. Its actual contents are not the relics that are preserved as the manger of Bethlehem. Its actual content is the Midnight Mass at the birth of Christ. Only there does the transition into reality finally occur. Only there have we reached the Christmas image that is no longer an image. Only when we let ourselves be led there from the message of the room do the words hold true anew: Today a Savior is born to you. Yes, really today.

He goes on to consider the popular image of Mary, Salus Populi Romani:

In the drama of salvation it is not the case that Mary had a part to play before exiting the stage like an actor who has said his lines and departs. The Incarnation from the woman is not a role that is completed after a short time; rather, it is the abiding being of God with the earth, with men, with us who are earth. That is the reason why Christmas is at the same time both a feast of Mary and a feast of Christ, and for this reason a proper Nativity church must be a Marian church. We should view with the same thoughts the ancient, mysterious image that the Romans call *Salus Populi Romani.* According to tradition it is the image that Gregory the Great in 590 carried in a procession through the streets of Rome as the plague tortured the city. At the conclusion of the procession the pestilence ended, and Rome was again healthy. The name of the image means to say to us that man can become healthy again and again from Rome. The maternal goodness of God looks out at us from this at once youthful and time-honored figure, from its knowing and kindly eyes. "As one whom his mother comforts, so I will comfort you," God says to us through the prophet Isaiah (66:13). God apparently prefers to accomplish maternal consolation through the mother, through his mother, and who could be surprised at this? Self-righteousness falls from us before this image. The tenseness of our pride, the fear of feeling, and everything that makes us internally ill dissolve. Depression and despair result when the balance of our feelings becomes disordered or even suspended. We no longer see the warmth, the consolation, the goodness, and the salutariness of the world, everything that we can perceive only with our hearts. The world becomes despair in the coldness of knowledge that has lost its roots. For this reason, acceptance of this image cures. It gives us back the earth of faith and humanity when we accept its language interiorly and do not close ourselves to it.

The interaction of arch of triumph and cave teaches us to pass from aesthetics to faith, as we said before. The transition to this image can lead us a step farther still. It helps us to loosen faith from the strain of will and intellect and allow it to enter into the whole of our existence. It gives aesthetics back to us in a new and greater way: if we have followed the call of the Savior, we can also receive anew the language of the earth, which he himself assumed. We may open ourselves to the closeness of the mother without fear of falling into false sentimentality or myth. It only becomes mythic or sick when we tear it away from the great context of the mystery of Christ. Then, what has been pushed aside comes back as something esoteric in confused forms whose promise is empty and deceptive. The true consolation appears in the image of the Mother of the Savior. God is near enough for us to touch him, even today. If, in our watchful stay in this church, we become aware of this consolation, then its saving and transforming message has entered into us.

Joseph Cardinal Ratzinger, "The Message of the Basilica of Saint Mary Major in Rome," in *Images of Hope: Meditations on Major Feasts*, trans. John Rock and Graham Harrison (San Francisco: Ignatius Press, 2006), 18, 19, 20, 21–22.

Reflection Questions

❖ Cardinal Ratzinger, Pope Benedict XVI, links art to a deeper contemplation of the mysteries of the faith. How does my appreciation for religious art assist my prayer life, especially contemplation?

❖ Do I appreciate the relationship that exists between the Virgin Mary and the Church?

Solemnity of the Assumption of the Blessed Virgin Mary

Readings

Vigil Mass
1 Chronicles 15:3–4, 15–16; 16:1–2; 1 Corinthians 15:54b–57; Luke 11:27–28

Day of the Feast
Revelation 11:19a; 12:1–6a, 10; 1 Corinthians 15:20–27; Luke 1:39–56

Historical Note

According to theologian Danilo Sartor, OSM, the feast of the Assumption of the Blessed Virgin Mary was first celebrated in sixth-century Jerusalem. The Emperor Maurice (582–602) ordered the celebration of the Assumption for the entire empire In the Byzantine Empire, it was called the "Dormition" (*koimesis*/falling asleep) of the Blessed Virgin Mary. By the late seventh century, during the time of Pope Sergius I (687–701), four Marian feasts were celebrated in Rome: the Nativity of the Virgin Mary, the Annunciation, the Purification, and the Assumption. On these feasts a solemn procession was held through the streets of the city, ending at the Basilica of St. Mary Major. From Rome, the feast of the Assumption spread quickly in the West. In 1950, having studied the petitions that had been arriving in Rome since the nineteenth century from the lay faithful, and after a formal consultation with the world's bishops, Pope Pius XII defined the Assumption as a dogma. He issued an Apostolic Constitution, *Munificentissimus Deus* (November 1, 1950). In it he wrote:

... by the authority of our Lord Jesus Christ, of the blessed apostles Peter and Paul, and by our own authority, we proclaim, declare and define as a dogma revealed by God: the Immaculate Mother of God, Mary ever Virgin, when the course of her earthly life was ended, was taken up body and soul into the glory of heaven.

> Pope Pius XII, *Munificentissimus Deus*, in *The Christian Faith*, ed. Jacques Dupuis, 7th rev. ed. (New York: Alba House, 2001), 287.

Pope John Paul II, in his encyclical letter Redemptoris Mater, *included the doctrine of the Assumption in the section on Mary's maternal mediation:*

Through her mediation, subordinate to that of the Redeemer, Mary contributes *in a special way to the union of the pilgrim Church* on earth with the eschatological and heavenly *reality* of the Communion of Saints, since she has already been "assumed into heaven." The truth of the Assumption, defined by Pius XII, is reaffirmed by the Second Vatican Council, which thus expresses the Church's faith: "Preserved free from all guilt of original sin, the Immaculate Virgin *was taken up body and soul into heavenly glory* upon the completion of her earthly sojourn. She was *exalted* by the Lord *as Queen of the Universe*, in order that she might be the more thoroughly conformed to her Son, the Lord of lords (cf. Rev. 19:16) and the conqueror of sin and death." In this teaching Pius XII was in continuity with Tradition, which has found many different expressions in the history of the Church, both in the East and in the West.

By the mystery of the Assumption into heaven there were definitively accomplished in Mary all the effects of the one mediation of *Christ the Redeemer of the world* and *Risen Lord*. "In Christ shall all be made alive. But each in his own order: Christ the first fruits, then at his coming those who belong to Christ" (1 Cor 15:22–23). In the mystery of the Assumption is expressed the faith of the Church, according to which Mary is "united by a close and indissoluble bond" to Christ, for, if as Virgin and Mother she was singularly united with him *in his first coming*, so through her continued collaboration with him she will also be united with him in expectation of the second; "redeemed in an especially sublime manner by reason of the merits of her Son," she also has that specifically maternal role of mediatrix of mercy *at his final coming*, when all those who belong to Christ "shall be made alive," when "the last enemy to be destroyed is death" (1 Cor 15:26).

Connected with this exaltation of the noble "Daughter of Sion" through her Assumption into heaven is the mystery of her eternal glory. For the Mother of Christ is glorified as "Queen of the Universe." She who at the Annunciation called herself the "handmaid of the Lord" remained throughout her earthly life faithful to what this name expresses. In this she confirmed that she was a true "disciple" of Christ, who strongly emphasized that his mission was one of service: the Son of Man "came not to be served but to serve, and to give his life as a ransom for many" (Mt 20:28). In this way Mary became the first of those who, "serving Christ also in others, with humility and patience lead their brothers and sisters to that King whom to serve is to reign," and she fully obtained that "state of royal freedom" proper to Christ's disciples: to serve means to reign!

"Christ obeyed even at the cost of death, and was therefore raised up by the Father (cf. Phil 2:8–9). Thus he entered into the glory of his kingdom. To him all things are made subject until he subjects himself and all created things to the Father, that God may be all in all (cf. 1 Cor 15:27–28)." Mary, the handmaid of the Lord, has a share in this Kingdom of the Son. The *glory of serving* does not cease to be her royal exaltation: assumed into heaven, she does not cease her saving service, which expresses her maternal mediation "until the eternal fulfillment of all the elect." Thus, she who here on earth "loyally persevered in her union with her Son unto the Cross," continues to remain united with him, while now *"all things are subjected to him, until he subjects to the Father himself and all things."* Thus in her Assumption into heaven, Mary is as it were clothed by the whole reality of the Communion of Saints, and her very union with the Son in glory is wholly oriented toward the definitive fullness of the Kingdom, *when "God will be all in all."*

In this phase too Mary's maternal mediation does not cease to be subordinate to him who is the one Mediator, *until the final realization of "the fullness of time,"* that is to say until "all things are united in Christ" (cf. Eph 1:10).

Pope John Paul II, *Redemptoris Mater*, no. 41.

Caryll Houselander, in the concluding chapter of her work The Reed of God, *offers a meditation on the Assumption of the Blessed Virgin Mary.*

In heaven Our Lady is with God.

Our Lady's body is there, and the Body of Christ is there: and our lady's soul and the soul of Christ and His divinity.

We can realize this only in so far as we realize it through its effect upon the world.

There, before God, is humanity, our humanity; but innocent humanity in all its primal loveliness; humanity with which the Spirit of God is in love.

And she is ours!

Therefore, it is always Advent, always spring: the life and birth and death and resurrection of Christ always goes on upon earth, an unending circle of light.

Because even now, and always, the *fiat* is uttered, and the Love of the Spirit of Life is consummated in the Child

Bride; the earth is continually made new; we are continually born again.

This is what really matters most of all to everyone: the power to be made new.

Not simply beginning again, dragging along with the old scars, the old crippling wounds, the old weakness dragging at the will; limping with the weariness of yesterday, sore with the heartsickness of the last defeat, bitter with the still smarting grievance against one another.

Not that, but real newness, being born again.

A new will, new heart, new vision, new love—indeed new life.

Even in natural things, it is newness that gives us most delight: daybreak, morning in spring. These seem to us like promises from heaven, promises of our own renewal.

"I will give you the morning star."

To be born again: that is exactly what Christ has promised to us; not only once, but just as often as our inner life grows old and jaded and dies.

But newness, flowering spring, shadowless morning, are not born of what is decaying, corrupt and fetid.

They are born only of virginity, virginity which *is* newness, virginity complete as fire and water.

The only virginity like that is the virginity of Our Lady; it is through this virginity that the earth is made new, that the Holy Spirit is wed to humanity.

Through Mary of Nazareth Christ is born again and again in the individual heart.

"Blessed is the fruit of thy womb, Jesus," the little children say. And they do not understand what they say. But as they grow older, with the angel's prayer in their hearts, they begin to understand that this "fruit" is the Life of Christ born again in the world—always, everywhere.

Our Lady is in heaven.

On earth the breath of the spirit is stirring the young green corn. The song of the shepherd is heard in lambing time.

In heaven the music of the Incarnation is uttered eternally in its first simplicity.

The Mother has found the lost Child.

The empty Chalice is brimming with wine.

The Reed is filled with infinite music....

Caryll Houselander, *The Reed of God*, 127–28.

Reflection Questions

❖ The solemnity of the Assumption of the Blessed Virgin Mary is a feast of great hope and consolation. It affirms the goodness of all God's creation and invites us to reflect on our care of God's earth, especially on the dignity and beauty of the human body. Our bodies are temples of the Holy Spirit. Do we treat our bodies and the bodies of others with proper respect and reverence?

❖ The solemnity of the Assumption asks us to keep our eyes on the final goal: heaven. There we will be united, body and soul, with the risen Jesus, the Blessed Mother, and the "great cloud of witnesses" (Heb 12:1), all those saints and family members who have gone before us into the fullness of eternal life. Do the choices we make in life reflect our *desire* to reach heaven?

Feast of the Queenship
of the Blessed Virgin Mary

Readings

No readings are assigned to this feast. The readings may come from the lectionary cycle for Ordinary Time, or from the Common of Masses of the Blessed Virgin Mary.

Historical Note

The 1950s marked a time of intense theological debate among theologians concerning the Church's understanding of the Blessed Virgin Mary. In 1950, Pope Pius XII defined the mystery of the Assumption of Mary as a dogma.

In 1954, to commemorate the centennial anniversary of the dogma of the Immaculate Conception, he proclaimed a Marian year. In that same year, he wrote an encyclical letter *Ad Caeli Reginam* (Queen of Heaven) in which he presented a theological basis for the recognition of this title, and established a feast of the Queenship of Mary to be celebrated on May 31. In the liturgical reform of 1969, the feast was transferred to August 22.

Dante Alighieri (1265–1321), in his classic poem the Divine Comedy, *traces the spiritual journey from conversion to its ultimate goal: participation in the beatific vision. The poem is divided into three main parts: inferno (hell), purgatory, and paradise. In the final canto (paradise), St. Bernard of Clairvaux leads Dante (every pilgrim) to the "empyrean" where the sojourner hears Bernard implore the intercession of the Blessed Virgin Mary, Queen of heaven and earth. Bernard's prayer is a masterpiece of literary eloquence and theological depth concerning his understanding of Mary's place in the economy of salvation. Dante writes:*

"Virgin Mother, daughter of thy son;
humble beyond all creatures and more exalted;
predestined turning point of God's intention;

thy merit so ennobled human nature
that its divine Creator did not scorn
to make Himself the creature of His creature.

The Love that was rekindled in Thy womb
sends forth the warmth of the eternal peace
within whose ray this flower has come to bloom.

Here, to us, thou art the noon and scope
of Love revealed; and among mortal men,
the living fountain of eternal hope.

Lady, that art so near God's reckonings
that who seeks grace and does not first seek thee
would have his wish fly upward without wings.

Not only does thy sweet benignity
flow out to all who beg, but oftentimes
thy charity arrives before the plea.

In thee is pity, in thee munificence,
in thee the tenderest heart, in thee unites
all that creation knows of excellence!

Now come this man who from the final pit
of the universe up to this height has seen,
one by one, the three lives of the spirit.

He prays to thee in fervent supplication
for grace and strength, that he may raise his eyes
to the all-healing final revelation.

And I, who never more desired to see
the vision myself than I do that he may see It,
add my own prayer, and pray that it may be

enough to move you to dispel the trace
of every mortal shadow by thy prayers
and let him see revealed the Sum of Grace.

I pray thee further, all-persuading Queen,
keep whole the natural bent of his affections
and of his powers after his eyes have seen.

Protect him from the stirrings of man's clay;
see how Beatrice and the blessed host
clasp reverent hands to join me as I pray."

The eyes that God reveres and loves the best
Glowed on the speaker, making clear the joy
With which true prayer is heard by the most blest.

Dante Alighieri, Canto XXXIII:1–42,
of "The Paradiso," in *Divine Comedy*, trans. John Ciardi
(New York: Signet/Mentor, 1961), 360–62.

Pope Pius XII (1939–1958) in his encyclical letter Ad Caeli Reginam (Proclaiming the Queenship of Mary) *traces the history of the recognition of the Queenship of Mary in the Catholic tradition. He identifies those sources where one can find a consistent belief in Mary's Queenship as participation in the royal dignity of her Son. These sources include the writings of saints, theologians, and popes; the sacred liturgy of East and West; the Litany of Loreto, the Fifth Glorious Mystery of the Rosary, and sacred art. The Pope expresses the formal theological principle thus:*

[A]ccording to ancient tradition and the scared liturgy the main principle on which the royal dignity of Mary rests is without doubt her Divine Motherhood. In Holy Writ, concerning the Son whom Mary will conceive, we read this sentence: "He shall be called the Son of the most High, and the Lord God shall give unto him the throne of David his father, and he shall reign in the house of Jacob forever, and of his kingdom there will be no end," and in addition Mary is called "Mother of the Lord"; from this it is easily concluded that she is a Queen, since she bore a son who, at the very moment of His conception, because of the hypostatic union of the human nature with the Word, was also as man King and Lord of all things. So with complete justice St. John Damascene could write: "When she became Mother of the Creator, she truly became Queen of every creature."

In the concluding words of the encyclical, the Pope also added the importance of recognizing Mary under the title of Queen of Peace:

We are convinced that this feast will help to preserve, strengthen and prolong that peace among nations which daily is almost destroyed by recurring crises. Is she not a rainbow in the clouds reaching towards God, the pledge of a covenant of peace? ... Whoever, therefore, reverences the Queen of heaven and earth—and let no one consider himself exempt from this tribute of a grateful and loving soul—let him invoke the most effective of Queens, the Mediatrix of peace; let him respect and preserve peace, which is not wickedness unpunished nor freedom without restraint, but a well-ordered harmony under the rule of the will of God; to its safeguarding and growth the gentle urgings and commands of the Virgin Mary impel us.

Pope Pius XII, *Ad Caeli Reginam*, nos. 34 and 51 (October 11, 1954), in *The Papal Encyclicals 1939–1958*, Claudia Carlen, IHM (Raleigh: McGrath Publishing, 1981), 274, 277.

On March 25, 1981, the Congregation for the Sacraments and Divine Worship published the Order of Crowning an Image of the Blessed Virgin Mary. *Its English translation appeared in 1987. The document includes a theological reflection on the meaning of the Queenship of Mary, the liturgical context in which such a crowning should take place, and a new litany in honor of the Blessed Virgin Mary. The introduction offers a theological meditation on the meaning of veneration to the Queenship of Mary.*

Coronation is one form of reverence frequently shown to images of the Blessed Virgin Mary. But in the case of images depicting the Mother of God holding her Son in her arms, there is a crowning of both figures: in the rite the crown is placed on the Son's head first, then on the Mother's.

Both in the East and in the West the practice of depicting the Blessed Virgin Mary wearing a regal crown came into use in the era of the Council of Ephesus (A.D. 431). Since then Christian artists have often portrayed the glorified Mother of the Lord seated on a throne, dressed in royal robes, and surrounded by a court of angels and saints. In many such images Christ is shown placing a crown on his Mother's head.

It is especially from the end of the 16th century that in the West the practice became widespread for the faithful, both religious and laity, to crown images of the Blessed Virgin. The popes not only endorsed this devout custom but "on many occasions, either personally or through bishop-delegates, carried out the coronation of Marian images."

The growth of the custom led to the composition of a special rite for crowning images of Mary, and in the 19th century this was incorporated into the Roman liturgy.

By means of this rite the Church proclaims that the Blessed Virgin Mary is rightly regarded and invoked as queen for the following reasons.

She is the Mother of the Son of God, who is the messianic King. Mary is the Mother of Christ, the Word Incarnate, in whom "all things were created, in heaven and on earth, visible and invisible, whether thrones or dominations or principalities or authorities." She is the Mother of the Son of David, and of him the angels said in prophecy: "He will be great and will be called the Son of the Most High; and the Lord God will give him the throne of his father David; and he will reign over the house of Jacob for ever; and of his kingdom there will be no end." Thus, filled with the Holy Spirit, Elizabeth greeted Mary, pregnant with Jesus, as "the Mother of my Lord."

She is the chosen companion of the Redeemer. By God's eternal plan, the Blessed Virgin Mary, the new Eve, had an altogether special part in the work of the redemption, by which Christ, the new Adam, redeemed us and made us his own, not with perishable things such as silver and gold, but with his precious blood, and has made us a kingdom to our God.

She is the perfect follower of Christ. The maid of Nazareth consented to God's plan; she journeyed on the pilgrimage of faith; she listened to God's word and kept it in her heart; she remained steadfastly in close union with her Son, all the way to the foot of the cross; she persevered in prayer with the Church. Thus in an eminent way she won the "crown of righteousness," the "crown of life," the "crown of glory" that is promised to those who follow Christ. And "upon the completion of her earthly sojourn, she was taken up body and soul into heavenly glory and was exalted by the Lord as Queen of all, in order that she might be more completely conformed to her Son, the Lord of lords and the victor over death."

She is the foremost member of the Church. The handmaid of the Lord, in whom ancient Israel had its culmination and the new people of God its holy beginning, is "the greatest, best, principal, and finest part" of the Church. Because of the singular charge entrusted to her with respect to Christ and the members of his mystical Body and because of her richness in virtue and fullness of grace, she who is blessed among women is preeminent in the Church, this chosen race, this royal priesthood, this holy nation. She is therefore rightly invoked as Queen of angels and of saints, as our Lady and our Queen. The glory of Mary, who is a daughter of Adam and sister to us all, not only does honor to the people of God, but ennobles the entire human family.

Congregation for the Sacraments and Divine Worship, "Introduction," in *Order of Crowning an Image of the Blessed Virgin Mary*, in *The Rites of the Catholic Church as Revised by the Second Vatican Ecumenical Council*, vol. 2, study ed. (Collegeville, MN: Pueblo Book/Liturgical Press, 1991), nos. 2–5, pp. 454–55.

The Order of Crowning *also includes a new litany to the Blessed Virgin Mary. The litany retained some of the invocations of the Queenship of Mary as found in the Litany of Loreto while introducing new ones:*

　Queen of love
　Queen of mercy
　Queen of peace
　Queen of angels
　Queen of patriarchs and prophets
　Queen of apostles and martyrs
　Queen of confessors and virgins
　Queen of all saints
　Queen conceived without original sin

Queen assumed into heaven
Queen of all the earth
Queen of heaven
Queen of the universe

> Congregation for the Sacraments and Divine Worship,
> *Order of Crowning, in Rites of the Catholic Church*, 476–77.

One of the most popular prayers that affirms the Queenship of Mary is the early medieval antiphon Regina Caeli *(Queen of Heaven). This text replaces the Angelus in the Easter season. It is also an option found in the* Liturgy of the Hours *to be used at the conclusion of Night Prayer during the Easter season.*

Queen of Heaven, rejoice, alleluia:
For the Son thou wast privileged to bear, alleluia,
Is risen, as he said, alleluia.
Pray for us to God, alleluia.

V. Rejoice and be glad, O Virgin Mary, alleluia!
R. For the Lord is truly risen, alleluia.

> (*Liturgy of the Hours*, Night Prayer for the Season of Easter)

Let us pray: O God, who gave joy to the world through the Resurrection of thy Son our Lord Jesus Christ, grant, we beseech thee, that through the intercession of the Virgin

Mary, his Mother, we may obtain the joys of everlasting life. Through the same Christ our Lord. Amen.

(*Roman Missal*, collect from the
Common of the B.V.M. during the Easter Season)

Regina Caeli, in Manual of Indulgences. Translation into English
from the fourth edition (1999) of *Enchiridion Indulgentiarum
Normae et Concessiones* (Washington, DC: United States Conference
of Catholic Bishops, 2006), 60.

Reflection Question

❖ How have the theological and devotional aspects of these reflections made me more aware of the significance of this feast?

Feast of the Birth
of the Blessed Virgin Mary

Readings

Micah 5:1–4 or Romans 8:28–30; Matthew 1:1–16, 18–23

Historical Note

The Gospels do not tell us the names of Mary's parents or any other details concerning her birth. In the *Protoevangelium of James*, a late second-century apocryphal work that captured the imagination of the era but was not concerned with the presentation of scientific history, we learn the names her parents were Joachim and Anne. Their feast is celebrated on July 26. The feast of the birth of the Blessed Virgin is traced back to sixth-century Jerusalem, to a church consecrated to the memory of St. Anne. It is believed that this church, the present-day Basilica of St. Anne, was built over the house where Mary was born. The feast was celebrated in Rome by the seventh century, and is now celebrated in both East and West. The date of the feast varied over the centuries until the feast of the Immaculate Conception was fixed on December 8. The feast of Mary's birth was then established on September 8, nine months after the feast of the Immaculate Conception.

St. Andrew of Crete (c. 660–c. 740) was one of the truly outstanding homilists and poets from the Patristic era. Born in Damascus, he served as a monk in the city of Jerusalem until his election as the archbishop of Crete. Besides his writings on the Blessed Virgin Mary, St. Andrew staunchly defended the veneration of icons and greatly influenced the spirituality of Eastern Christianity. This text is taken from the Office of Readings for the feast of the Birth of Mary.

... The present festival, the birth of the Mother of God, is the prelude, while the final act is the foreordained union of the Word with flesh. Today the Virgin is born, tended and formed, and prepared for her role as Mother of God, who is the universal King of the ages.

Justly then do we celebrate this mystery since it signifies for us a double grace. We are led toward the truth, and we are led away from our condition of slavery to the letter of the law. How can this be? Darkness yields before the coming of light, and grace exchanges legalism for freedom. But midway between the two stands today's mystery, at the frontier where types and symbols give way to reality, and the old is replaced by the new.

Therefore, let all creation sing and dance and unite to make worthy contribution to the celebration of this day. Let there be one common festival for saints in heaven and men on earth. Let everything, mundane things and those above, join in festive celebration. Today this created world is raised to the dignity of a holy place for him who made all things. The creature is newly prepared to be a divine dwelling place for the Creator.

St. Andrew of Crete, *The Liturgy of the Hours*, Vol. IV
(New York: Catholic Book Publishing Co., 1975), 1371.

St. Bernard of Clairvaux (1090–1153) is a Doctor of the Church whose Marian teaching is found mainly in his sermons. He often spoke of the place of the Virgin Mary in the mystery of Christ and the mystery of the Church. On the feast of Mary's Nativity, he delivered a famous sermon on Mary as the "Aqueduct" through whom the grace of Christ flows. St. Bernard's clear teaching about Mary's mediation as found in the sermon would later exercise an enormous influence in Catholic theology and spirituality.

Now what is this fountain of life if it be not Christ the Lord? ... For the "Fountain is conveyed abroad" in a stream even to us; its waters flow "in the streets," although "the stranger partake not of them" (Prov 5:16, 17). This stream from the heavenly source descends to us through an Aqueduct; it does not indeed exhibit all the fullness of the Fountain, but it serves to moisten our dry and withered hearts with some few drops of the waters of grace, giving more to one, less to another. The Aqueduct itself is always full, so that all may receive of its fullness (John 1:16), yet not the fullness itself....

You have already divined, dearest brethren, unless I mistake, to whom I allude under the image of an Aqueduct which, receiving the fullness of the Fountain from the Father's heart, has transmitted the same to us, if not as it is in itself, at least in so far as we could contain it. Yea, for you know to whom it was said, "Hail, full of grace" (Luke 2:28). But shall we not wonder how such and so great a Conduit could have been formed, the top of which—like the ladder which Jacob saw in a vision (Gen 28:12)—was to reach to heaven, nay, to be lifted higher than the heavens, and to touch that Living Fountain of "the waters that are above the heavens" (Ps 148:4)?

Let us, therefore, look more deeply into this matter, and let us see with what sentiments of tender devotion the Lord would have us honor Mary, in whom He has placed the plenitude of all good; so that if there is anything of hope in us, if anything of grace, if anything of salvation, we may feel assured it has overflowed unto us from her who "went up from the desert flowing with delights" (Cant 8:5). Oh, truly may we call her a garden of delights, which the Divine "South Wind" not merely "comes and blows upon" (Cant 4:16), but comes down into and blows through, causing its aromatical spices, that is, the precious gifts of heavenly grace, to flow out and to be diffused abroad on every side. Remove from the heavens the material sun which enlightens the world, and what becomes of the day? Remove Mary, remove this Star of the sea, of life's "great and spacious sea" (Ps

103:25), and what is left us but a cloud of involving gloom, and "the shadow of death" (Job 10:22), and a darkness of exceeding dense?

Therefore, my dearest brethren, with every fibre, every feeling of our hearts, with all the affections of our minds, and with all the ardour of our souls, let us honor Mary, because such is the will of God, Who would have us to obtain everything through the hands of Mary....

Wherefore then should we desire anything else? My brethren, let us seek grace and let us seek it through Mary. Through Mary, I say, because she always finds what she seeks and can never suffer a disappointment. Yes, let us seek grace, but "grace with God," for with men "grace is deceitful" (Prov 30:31). Others may seek after merit, but let it be our endeavor to find grace....

But, my brother, whatsoever thou hast a mind to offer to the Lord be sure to entrust it to Mary, so that thy gift shall return to the Giver of all grace through the same channel by which thou didst obtain it. God of course had the power, if He so pleased, to communicate His grace without the interposition of this Aqueduct. But he wanted to provide us with a needful intermediary. For perhaps, "thy hands are full of blood" (Is 1:15) or dirtied with bribes: perhaps thou hast not like the Prophet "shaken them free from all gifts" (Is 30:15). Consequently, unless thou wouldst have thy gift rejected, be careful to commit to Mary the little thou desirest to offer, that the Lord may receive it through her hands, so dear to Him and most "worthy of all acceptation" (1 Tm 1:15). For Mary's hands are the very whitest of lilies; and assuredly the

Divine Lover of lilies will never complain of anything presented by His Mother's hands that is not found among the
lilies. Amen.

St. Bernard of Clairvaux, "Sermon for the Feast of the Nativity of the
Blessed Virgin Mary," in *St. Bernard's Sermons for the Seasons and
Principal Festivals of the Year*, trans. a priest of Mount Melleray, vol. III
(Westminster, ME: Carroll Press, 1950), 284, 285, 287, 288, 305.

*Rainer Maria Rilke (1875–1926) has been recognized as one of the
most influential poets of the twentieth century. He was born in Prague
and he died near Montreux, Switzerland. His childhood years were
difficult, often marked by periods of isolation. While he never completed his formal education, he dedicated his life to literature. He traveled throughout Europe, married and separated from his wife, and
worked for a time as a secretary to the famous French sculptor Auguste
Rodin (1840–1917). His writing reflects his knowledge of Catholic
philosophy and theology, biblical imagery, and his desire to find a very
personal God. In her work* Pictures of God, *Annemarie S. Kidder,
PhD, studied select poems by Rilke that explore his understanding of
certain components of religious faith, including the poem "The Life of
the Virgin Mary." Rilke wrote this work in 1912 while staying in
Duino, Italy.*

THE BIRTH OF MARY

(The Life of the Virgin Mary, 1912)

How must the angels have struggled
not to erupt in praises, like one might erupt in tears,
the minute they knew that tonight would be born

the mother, who'd soon bear the son.

Wings a-flapping they held their tongues pointing the
    direction
to where the only house was that of Joachim's;
o, how they could feel in the air the purest complexion,
but none was allowed to stoop down to him.

For the couple were already upset enough.
A neighbor had come to share what she barely knew,
and the old man had silenced a cow that mooed
as a precaution—and all seemed new.

Rainer Maria Rilke, "The Birth of Mary," in *Pictures of God: Rilke's
Religious Poetry, Including "The Life of the Virgin Mary,"* trans. Annemarie
S. Kidder (Livonia, MI: First Page Publications, 2005), 28.

Reflection Questions

❖ How does this feast help me to appreciate Mary's own
   growth within her family? How important is the role of
   parents and grandparents in the transmission of the faith,
   the passing on of stories of faith?

❖ Do I keep my own birthday and the birthdays of people
   important to me, as special gifts in my relationship with
   God?

Feast of the Most Holy Name of the Blessed Virgin Mary

Readings

No readings are assigned to this feast. The readings may come from the lectionary cycle for Ordinary Time, or from the Common of Masses of the Blessed Virgin Mary.

Historical Note

On September 8, the Church celebrated the birthday of Mary. Today, she invokes the powerful intercession of the Mother of the Church and the Mother of God in behalf of her children. This feast was initially introduced in Spain in the early sixteenth century. However, Pope Innocent XI (1676–1689) promoted it for the universal Church to mark the military victory of Christian forces over the Turks in 1683 at Vienna, Austria. In the biblical and ancient world, people's names revealed something about their personality and their divinely appointed mission in life. The Church recalls the brief yet powerful reference to Mary's name at the moment of the Annunciation (Lk 1: 27, "... and the virgin's name was Mary"). The angel invited Mary to consent to God's desire that she bear in her heart and in her womb the Savior of the world. The feast, which had been dropped from the liturgical calendar, was restored to the calendar in the revised *Missale Romanum, editio typica tertia* (March 2002).

St. Alphonsus Maria de Liguori reflects on the sweetness of the name of Mary in his work The Glories of Mary, *as the final meditation on the Salve Regina. St. Alphonsus recalls the ways in which theologians, preachers, and writers have appealed to her holy name, and concludes with a prayer to the Virgin Mary.*

The enamored St. Bernard, raising his heart to his good Mother, says, with tenderness, "O great! O pious! O you, who are worthy of all praise! O most Holy Virgin Mary! Your name is so sweet and amiable, that it cannot be pronounced without inflaming those who do so with love toward you and God. It only need occur to the thought of your lovers to move them to love you more, and to console them." ... "Your most sweet name, O Mary," according to St. Ambrose, "is a precious ointment, which breathes forth the odor of divine grace." The Saint then prays to the Divine Mother, saying: "Let this ointment of salvation enter the inmost recesses of our souls": that is, grant, O Lady, that we may often remember to name thee with love and confidence; for this practice either shows the possession of divine grace, or else is a pledge that we shall soon recover it.

On the other hand, Thomas à Kempis affirms, "that the devils fear the Queen of Heaven to such a degree, that on only hearing her great name pronounced, they fly from him who does so as from a burning fire." The Blessed Virgin herself revealed to Saint Bridget "that there is not on earth a sinner, however devoid he may be of the love of God, from whom the devil is not obliged immediately to fly, if he invokes her holy name with a determination to repent." On another occasion she repeated the same thing to the Saint, saying, "that all the devils venerate and fear her name to such a degree, that on hearing it they immediately loosen the claws with which they hold the soul captive." ...

PRAYER

O great Mother of God and my Mother Mary, it is true that I am unworthy to name you; but you, who loves me and desires my salvation, must, notwithstanding the impurity of my tongue, grant that I may always invoke your most holy and powerful name in my aid, for your name is the succor of the living, and the salvation of the dying. Most pure Mary, most sweet Mary, grant that from henceforth your name may be the breath of my life. O Lady, delay not to help me when I invoke you, for in all the temptations which assail me, and in all my wants, I will never cease calling upon thee, and repeating again and again, Mary, Mary. Thus it is that I hope to act during my life, and more particularly at death, that after that last struggle I may eternally praise your beloved name in heaven, O clement, O loving, O sweet Virgin Mary. Mary, most amiable Mary, with what consolation, what sweetness, what confidence, what tenderness, is my soul penetrated in only naming, in only thinking of you! I thank my Lord and God, who, for my good, has given you a name so sweet and deserving of love, and at the same time so powerful....

My own dear Mary, O my beloved Jesus, may your most sweet names reign in my heart, and in all hearts. Grant that I may forget all others to remember, and always invoke, your adorable names alone. Jesus my Redeemer, and my Mother Mary, when the moment of death comes, in which I must breathe forth my soul and leave this world, deign, through your merits, to grant that I may then pronounce my last words, and that they may be, "*I love you, O Jesus; I love you, O Mary;* to you do I give my heart and my soul."

St. Alphonsus Maria de Liguori, *The Glories of Mary* (London: Burns, Oates & Washbourne, 1852), 237, 238, 239, 246–47.

Reflection Questions

❖ Do I recognize the sacredness of a name?

❖ Do I show proper reverence toward the names of God and the Blessed Virgin Mary?

❖ Do I celebrate the name days of saints within my own family?

SEPTEMBER 15

Feast of Our Lady of Sorrows

Readings

No readings are assigned to this feast. The readings may come from the lectionary cycle for Ordinary Time, or from the Common of Masses of the Blessed Virgin Mary.

Historical Note

Reflections on Mary at the foot of the Cross (Jn 19:25–27) can be traced back to the late fourth and early fifth centuries. Saints and theologians from both the East (St. Ephrem, Romanos the Melodist) and the West (Saints Ambrose and Bernard of Clairvaux) wrote hymns and preached sermons on the compassion of the sorrowful Virgin. In 1011, an oratory was dedicated in Germany to "St. Mary at the Cross." From the twelfth to the fourteenth centuries, devotion to the sorrows of Mary increased. It was often based on the Gospel encounter between Simeon and the Virgin Mary (Lk 2:34–35) at the presentation of Jesus in the Temple. New religious orders like the Franciscans and the Servites of Mary spread devotions centered on the sorrowful mother. In 1423, the provincial Council of Cologne established a local feast to honor the sorrows of Mary. Hymns such as the *Stabat Mater Dolorosa*, and popular devotions such as the *Sorrows of Mary* became very popular. In art, the image of the *Pietà* became widespread. Pope St. Pius X established the feast on the day following the feast of the Exaltation of the Holy Cross.

Father Gerald Vann, OP (1906–1963), a well-known English Dominican author, lecturer, and retreat master, in his work The Seven Swords *weaves a reflection on the sorrows of the Virgin Mary with illustrations from paintings by El Greco (1541–1614). In the Gospel scene at the foot of the cross, the final words of the dying Jesus to his Mother (Jn 19:26) constitute the fifth sword.*

When a hurt or a sorrow, a loss or a cross, is stated in words, the words seem to make the facts more real and cruel, more hard to bear: there is a flat finality about them—I am going away; I don't love you; She is dead—that is like the tolling of a knell in the mind and heart. Mary had been standing afar off; but now she drew near; and would he now at the end have a word to speak to his mother?

Yes, and it was concerned with her comfort, his friend's care of her; yet at the same time it drove the sword deeper because it drew her life with him to a close: he was leaving her. And yet this word of dereliction for her has at the same time been taken throughout the ages as the symbol for the grand, universal, enlargement of her vocation as mother:

her motherhood of men. Woman, behold thy son John: but with him also the whole race of men, thy sons because my brothers.

And her work now will be to care for and cherish them as she had cared for and cherished him; to help them to fulfill their vocations as she had helped him fulfill his....

Perhaps in this scene at the foot of the cross a double answer is given us. There must surely be, first of all, in Mary that same unbreakable concentration of attention that we saw on the road to Calvary. There was also, in the second place, the giving of this new duty, this new work: the mothering of humanity.

The concentration of gaze: we should not be slothful if we lived habitually and familiarly in his presence. If we refused to live on the surface of life, to float placidly in the conventionalized religious shallows: if we freed ourselves, at whatever cost, from the frenzied tempo of modern life and taught ourselves to be still, to pray; then, in that prayer-stillness we should begin to be aware of the distant horizons which give this world its meaning, and so to do the work of every day in God and with God and for God; and his companionship would vitalize our wills and free us from our sloth.

But then there is also the work for humanity. It is more difficult, as St. John pointed out, for a man to love God whom he seeth not than to love his brother whom he seeth.... In these days it is hardly possible for anyone to remain unaware of the desperate needs of the world; but to the Christian these needs must appear in an especially forcible and dramatic form. For Christianity points us through death to life, through darkness to light; but it would seem as though the world today were facing in exactly the opposite direction, as though deep down within there were the will-to-death, as though the world were dying because it wants to die.

Sometimes indeed you find this death-wish explicit and complete, expressed in individual—or race—suicide. More often you find it in a paralysis of the will, a despair which destroys initiative; and there is an expression of this in the breakdown of the structure and machinery of society, a break-down which goes very deep, so that the attempt to stem it by frenzied legislation and short-term policies is but tinkering; there is an expression of it too in the passive acceptance of encroaching totalitarianism; and there is an expression of it in the hatred of beauty and wisdom and all the things that bring life to the spirit. All these things are simply a cry to the dark gods of destruction, Crucify us, crucify us; and why is there this adoration of death? We know in our own lives that in so far as we give ourselves to pride and falsehood, cruelty and greed, we call down death and disintegration upon ourselves; but there is that in us which lusts after that disintegration, and it will conquer us unless we learn that life is to be found not in self-worship but in Love-worship, that our name is love. So it is with a society which refuses that lesson: it may go on per-haps for centuries living on the surface forgetting the deep places, content without God; but sooner or later the shell cracks, the hollowness is revealed, and there is nothing left but the mocking grin of despair.

But what if we ourselves, despite our Christianity, are in the same position? We must go back to this same scene on Calvary, and see again God's self-revelation there....

And so the first lesson is deepened and reinforced: we cannot let ourselves be desperate and despondent, because we must be conscious of God's enfolding arms, God's motherly care and understanding and sympathy. We know that God's wisdom will send trials and derelictions; but in the light of this lesson we know that they are sent only to be creative for us and in us; and that just as out of Mary's dereliction came this greatness and this glory, so too, out of our small tribulations can come in our small way a sharing in her work: an ability to have something of her wise and tender and perceptive care for the people or the things God gives us to cherish.

For us then only to try to take them when they come without bitterness, without gloom, as a way in which our egoism can be exorcised, our hearts liberated to live in God and share God's power. And then too we shall know in the end of the joy of the final outcome. A woman when she is in labour hath sorrow because her hour is come; but when she hath brought forth the child she remembereth not the anguish, for joy that a man is born into the world. Mary had brought him forth into life, and now on Golgotha she watched over his death, his journey into the other greater life, and soon her sorrow too would be turned into greater joy. So for us too, if only we have faith and courage enough: You now have sorrow, but I will see you again and your heart shall rejoice; and your joy no man shall take from you.

Gerald Vann, OP, *The Seven Swords*
(London: Sheed and Ward, 1953), 55, 56, 60–63.

Joyce Rupp (1943–) is a member of the Community of the Servants of Mary (Servites). Author of more than ten books on spirituality, she has also offered retreats and conferences throughout the world. She has served as associate vocation director for the Archdiocese of Omaha, and as vocation director for the Servants of Mary. Her work Your Sorrow Is My Sorrow *is based on the seven sorrows of the Blessed Virgin Mary. Her meditation on the sixth sorrow is a reflection on Mary's reception of the dead body of Jesus into her arms. Based on the biblical text of John 19, this image has stimulated the artistic imagination in the various depictions of the statue of the* Pietà.

Every life has its share of pain, struggle, and hard times. Mary's life was no different. The greatest hurt of Mary's life is artistically expressed in Michelangelo's marble masterpiece, the *Pietà*, from the Latin word meaning loyalty and devotion. In this sensual, visceral work of art we see the poignant image of a mother holding the torn and ravaged body of her executed son. Both Mary's strength and immense love are portrayed through the face and posture that Michelangelo gives to her. In the *Pietà*, Mary has large, broad shoulders and a wide, generous lap on which the dead body of her son rests. The *Pietà* is a powerful reminder of how much strength love can have and how much pain it can evoke.

Mary gathered the dead body of Jesus into her loving arms, embracing him as one embraces a beloved who has been through tremendous agony. She not only drew his dead body to herself; she drew a lifetime of love, and all that he had suffered, to her heart. His pain was inside of her. There was an immense oneness between the mother who sat there and the crucified son whose body lay on her lap.

Mary received Jesus as one who compassionately receives the pain of the world or one's own great desolation. She held him as one who holds the horror of human tragedy and dreadful grief. She embraced him as one who embraces the deepest love they have ever known. Mary receiving the dead body of her son becomes a metaphor for any one of us, man or woman, when we open the arms of our love to receive suffering and death into our lives. By that generous gesture, we become living *Pietàs*.

I can never be with the *Pietà* for very long before I begin to resonate with the sufferings of others. I see Mary as a symbol for my own life, believing that I, too, am meant to receive others in their deep distress. The son whom Mary holds is a symbol of the suffering people in my life who need someone to be with them when they are vulnerable, sorely troubled, and overwhelmed with the intensity of life's painful unfolding.

The *Pietà* is a strong image of compassion. The figure of this sorrowful mother reflects all those who weep and grieve as they hold their great loss and pain close to their hearts in a long, embracing farewell. When I gaze upon the *Pietà*, I see, not just Mary, but every person who has ever embraced and held the pain of another in the arms of their care. In Mary I see each of us, gathering to our hearts the weary and worn ones of the world. Never have we needed this inspiration more. Our world is filled with pain and distress. Everywhere there are hurting ones longing to be received with this kind of loving embrace.

We can understand the *Pietà* as a posture of our heart when we are caught in the grips of goodbye or when we are tending to others who are suffering grievously. The experience of the *Pietà* is everywhere in our world. Mary receiving the dead body of her son is every parent, of any age, who has suffered the loss of a child. Mary holding the crucified Jesus is every sorrowing person who embraces a loved one and bids a final farewell. Mary is everyone filled with anguish and sorrow who has held what has died in their life and wondered why it happened. . . .

The key word of this sixth sorrow of Mary is "receive," meaning "to take back." When Mary received the dead body of Jesus in her arms, she was taking back, receiving Jesus in his totality, with all the accompanying pain that came with holding his battered body. In that moment, Mary had come full circle with Jesus, receiving in death the bruised and beaten body of the son she had birthed as a fresh, healthy child some thirty-three years earlier. Everything she had known and cherished about her son, all the love they had shared, the trials and tribulations they had experienced, each hope and dream she had for him, all this Mary held on her sorrowing lap.

The wounded Christ in Mary's lap is also in the lap of our lives. The Jesus of the *Pietà* is each suffering person who enters our life. We may be receiving the dead body of someone we love or we may be receiving a nonphysical death (a great loss) that causes us, or someone else, immense grief. Being a living *Pietà* means that there are moments in life when we need to hold what has died, cherish what has been, and accept the reality of the pain that comes with this loss.

When we receive hurting ones, we gather them to our heart as Mary did and embrace them as a wounded Christ.

We cradle them with care and reverence in the lap of our compassion. A lap is that part of us that we naturally have when we sit down; it allows us the ability to hold things there. A lap is a place of comfort where little ones are cradled, where children feel sheltered and protected. It is while lying on the lap of the mother that the child is nurtured and often where children are rocked to sleep.

Mary's lap was spacious. We, too, need space—spiritual, emotional, mental, and physical,—in order to receive another's pain, to give our attention to it and embrace it. Sometimes suffering is shoved into our lap. We do not expect or want the experience of receiving it. We would not choose to have it plopped into our lap, but there it is, whether we desire it or not. We may feel forced into being a living *Pietà* by a life situation that cannot be avoided. At other times, we deliberately open the arms of our love to embrace the one who bears suffering. At these times, we feel called to reach out toward that person's suffering, to receive it as Mary received her son. We still find it difficult, but we choose to do it. Anytime we reach out with love toward another person's suffering, we are Mary receiving Jesus into her arms.

Joyce Rupp, *Your Sorrow Is My Sorrow*
(New York: Crossroad Publishing Company, 1999), 140–43.

SPEAKING TO MARY

Mary, you have been there before me.
You opened your arms, your lap,
to receive the body of your son.
His scourged and crucified flesh told you

of the sufferings he had endured.
You held him as beloved, wounded child,
with all the pain a mother's heart could have.
I, too, have known loss in my life.
Teach me how to embrace this suffering.
Remind me of your generous lap
and the broad strength of your shoulders.
As I receive what is wounded
may I hold it as lovingly
as you held your child, Jesus.
Woman of Compassion, Mother of Sorrows,
I draw inspiration from your journey.
I, too, can move through the pain of my present
situation.
Your faith and courage lead me to my own.

Joyce Rupp, *Your Sorrow Is My Sorrow*, 149.

Reflection Questions

❖ How does the compassion of Mary challenge me to be more compassionate to those who are suffering? Am I present to them?

❖ When suffering enters my life, or the lives of loved ones, do I turn to Mary for guidance in the discernment of God's will? Do I experience the tenderness of her maternal embrace?

Feast of Our Lady of the Rosary

Readings

No readings are assigned to this feast. The readings may come from the lectionary cycle for Ordinary Time, or from the Common of Masses of the Blessed Virgin Mary.

Historical Note

In its present form, the Rosary comes to us from the time of Pope St. Pius V (1566–1572). Following the naval victory of Christian forces over the Turks at the battle of Lepanto in 1571, Pope Pius V established the feast of Our Lady of Victory. Later popes changed the name of the feast to that of Our Lady of the Rosary and extended it to the universal Church. Popes from Gregory XIII (1572–1610) to Benedict XVI (2005–) have all praised and encouraged the use of the Rosary as an outstanding form of prayer for Catholics in every state of life. On October 16, 2002, Pope John Paul II, in an apostolic letter, *Rosarium Virginis Mariae*, once again reflected upon the power and contemplative value of the Rosary. He also introduced a new series of mysteries, the

Luminous Mysteries. This expansion meant the inclusion of a greater number of moments from the life of Christ.

Father Jerome M. Vereb, CP (1945–), is a Passionist priest, theologian, and author who has served on several theological faculties. He worked in the service of the Holy See at the Vatican during the pontificate of Pope John Paul II. Father Vereb's book Pope John Paul II and the Luminous Mysteries of the Rosary *offers many insights into the history of the Rosary and into its theological, anthropological, and devotional value. He also identifies Pope John Paul II's way of praying the Rosary.*

Pope John Paul II proposes a three-step technique for reciting the Rosary. The first of these is announcing each Mystery out loud, even if just to oneself, if convenient. The words themselves provide the focus. Like the visual images found in Catholic culture, such as the crucifix, icons, and statues, the words of the Mystery are intended to sharpen the attention and to recall the "composition of place," as already referred to above by citing the teaching of St. Ignatius Loyola. The Rosary is definitely about the appeal to the senses. The entire prayer of the Rosary invites a certain passivity so that one may *experience* the grace interiorly.

For pragmatic Americans this concept appears foreign. The English-speaking world is oriented toward accomplishment and therefore is utilitarian. However, Christianity is about the effectiveness of God's grace, and therefore we pray:

"May God who has begun this good work in us bring it to fulfillment."

The history of Christian spirituality is telling. Passivity is effective *only if one allows God to speak*. The Pope advises that without keeping this principle in mind the Rosary's continued repetition will only give rise to *ennui*, i.e., boredom, detachment, an "I don't care" attitude. In order to prevent this, Pope John Paul II recommends reading passages of Scripture in accompaniment with the presentation of each Mystery. This method, too, feeds the imagination and the intellect. It inspires insight. Insight comforts. The image of the whole Jesus-Mystery, God's intervention in human history and His action in Christ, is really at the heart of the prayer of the Rosary. The Rosary is an appreciation of God.

Finally, the Pope's method calls for silence. Here he is specific. Here he invites a pause after the Mystery has been announced and the biblical passage has been reviewed. This is a moment of focus, important in every human activity. The fruit of focus is effectiveness. For this cause, the Pope has specifically written: "A discovery of the importance of silence is one of the secrets of practicing contemplation and meditation. One drawback of a society dominated by technology and the mass media is the fact that silence becomes increasingly difficult to achieve. Just as moments of silence are recommended in the Liturgy, so too in the recitation of the Rosary it is fitting to pause briefly after listening to the Word of God, while the mind focuses on the content of a particular Mystery" (*RVM*, no. 31).

Because it relies on images, meditation points to poetry. At first the realization of this fact may prove daunting, but eventually it is a comfort. It is certainly the fulfillment of a biblical mandate: "Be filled with the Spirit, speaking to yourselves in songs, hymns, and spiritual psalms, singing and making melody in your heart" (Eph 5:19). Silence stirs up personal images. It can recall distractions, consolations, and desolations from one's past experience. It places everything before God: memorable moments of self-knowledge, affections of sorrow and love, conversations with the Divine Presence, and sometimes just simply no thoughts or feelings at all, a kind of emptiness which is an invitation to God to come and fill the void. An individual who is serious about his or her life, in perpetual quest to draw analogies from the everyday world, is no stranger to the recollection and silence which the Pope calls for.

Of course, all of this is expressed in the second panel of the *Ave Maria:* "Holy Mary, Mother of God, pray for us sinners now and at the hour of our death. Amen." One's actions, memories, and aspirations perpetually seek the mercy of God, which is always available from the intercession of Jesus, accompanied by the prayers of Mary.

Jerome M. Vereb, CP, *Pope John Paul II and the Luminous Mysteries of the Rosary* (NJ: Catholic Book Publishing Co., 2003), 91–93.

Caryll Houselander responded to Maisie Ward's request for prayers to accompany each of the mysteries of the Rosary. Ward's book on the Rosary included the biblical text for each mystery, her own reflection, the copy of a work of art by Fra Angelico (1387–1455), and the prayers

composed by Caryll Houselander. In her introduction, Ward noted how Houselander wrote some of the prayers while she was lying flat on her back as London was being bombed during World War II. This excerpt records her prayers for each Joyful Mystery of the Rosary.

1. The Annunciation
Descend, Holy Spirit of Life!
Come down into our hearts,
that we may live.
Descend into emptiness,
that emptiness
may be filled.
Descend into the dust,
that the dust may flower.
Descend into the dark,
that the light
may shine in darkness.

2. The Visitation
Breath of Heaven,
carry us on the impulse
of Christ's love,
as easily as thistledown
is carried on the wind;
that in the Advent season of our souls,
while He is formed in us,
in secret and in silence—
the Creator
in the hands of His creatures,
as the Host
in the hands of the priest—

we may carry him forth
to wherever He wishes to be,
as Mary carried Him over the hills
on His errand of love,
to the house of Elizabeth.

3. The Nativity
Be born in us,
Incarnate Love.
Take our flesh and blood,
and give us Your humanity;
take our eyes, and give us Your vision;
take our minds,
and give us Your pure thought;
take our feet and set them in Your path;
take our hands
and fold them in Your prayer;
take our hearts
and give them Your will to love.

4. The Presentation
By the humility
of Jesus, Mary and Joseph
give us the glory of humility.
By the mystery
of innocence
obeying the law
binding upon sinners,
make us obedient.
By the offering of the poor,
the two white doves

in the gentle hands
of the pure Mother of Love,
give us the spirit of poverty.

5. The Finding in the Temple
Through Mary,
seeking her lost son,
may we be given grace
always to seek for the Christ-child
and always to find Him.
Let us find Him in all children,
and in all who have a child's needs—
the helpless, the sick, the simple,
the aged;
in all who serve
and are trusting and poor;
in all who are lonely or homeless.
Let us too become as little children,
to find the Divine Child
in our own hearts.

Maisie Ward, *Splendor of the Rosary*, 65, 73, 80, 87, 93.

Reflection Questions

❖ What is my experience of the Rosary?

❖ Do my reflections on each mystery allow me to reach a deeper understanding of the role of Mary as the Mother of God?

Feast of the Presentation of Mary

Readings

No readings are assigned to this feast. The readings may come from the lectionary cycle for Ordinary Time, or from the Common of Masses of the Blessed Virgin Mary.

Historical Note

This feast claims as its source the apocryphal *Protoevangelium of James*. It is a major feast in the Eastern and Orthodox Churches. The liturgical books of the Byzantine Church refer to it as "The Entrance of the *Theotokos* into the Temple." On November 21, 543, the Emperor Justinian (527–565) dedicated a church in Jerusalem to honor the Virgin Mary. The historical roots of this feast are found in this event. That church was destroyed in the following century during the Persian invasion. In the eighth century, the feast was established in Constantinople, and by the ninth century, it had spread to the West. It first took root there in Eastern monastic communities in southern Italy. In 1373, it was celebrated at the papal court in Avignon, France, and spread farther throughout the West. In 1568, however, Pope St. Pius V suppressed it as part of the Tridentine reform.

Later in the sixteenth century, the feast was restored to the liturgical calendar.

The Very Reverend Protopresbyter Thomas Hopko (1939–) is an Orthodox priest, theologian, lecturer, and author. From 1968 until 2002, he taught dogmatic theology at St. Vladimir's Seminary in Crestwood, New York. He served as president of the Orthodox Theological Society in America (1992–1995). A prolific writer, Father Hopko wrote the four-volume work, The Orthodox Faith: An Elementary Handbook on the Orthodox Church. *The second volume,* Worship, *includes a reflection on this feast.*

The second great feast of the *Theotokos* is the celebration of her entrance as a child into the Jerusalem Temple which is commemorated on the twenty-first of November. Like the feast of her nativity, this feast of Mary is without direct biblical and historical reference. But like the nativity, it is a feast filled with important spiritual significance for the Christian believer. The texts of the service tells how Mary was brought as a small child to the temple by her parents in order to be raised there among the virgins consecrated to the service of the Lord until the time of their betrothal in marriage. According to Church tradition, Mary was solemnly received by the temple community which was headed by the priest Zacharias, the father of John the Baptist. She was led to the holy place to be "nourished" there by the angels in order to become herself the "holy of holies" of God, the living sanctuary and temple of the Divine child who was to be born in her....

The main theme of the feast of Mary's entrance to the Temple, repeated many times in the liturgical services, is the fact that she enters the Temple to become herself the living temple of God, thus inaugurating the New Testament in which are fulfilled the prophecies of old that "the dwelling of God is with man" and that the human person is the sole proper dwelling place of the Divine Presence (Ezekiel 37:27; John 14:15–23; Acts 7:47; 2 Corinthians 6:11; Ephesians 2:18–22; 1 Peter 2:4; Revelation 22:1–4).

> Today is the preview of the good will of God, of the preaching of the salvation of mankind. The Virgin appears in the temple of God, in anticipation proclaiming Christ to all. Let us rejoice and sing to her: Rejoice, O Divine Fulfillment of the Creator's dispensation (*Troparion*).
>
> The most pure Temple of the Saviour, the precious Chamber and Virgin, the Sacred Treasure of the Glory of God, is presented today to the house of the Lord. She brings with her the grace of the Spirit, which the angels of God do praise. Truly this woman is the Abode of Heaven! (*Kontakion*).

Thus, the feast of the Entrance of the *Theotokos* into the Temple is the feast which celebrates the end of the physical temple in Jerusalem as the dwelling place of God. When the child Mary enters the Temple, the time of the temple comes to an end and the "preview of the good will of God" is shown forth. On this feast we celebrate—in the person of Christ's mother—that we too are the house and tabernacle of the Lord.

Father Thomas Hopko, *The Orthodox Faith: An Elementary Handbook on the Orthodox Church*, vol. II, *Worship* (New York: Department of Religious Education of the Orthodox Church in America, 1976), 141, 142, 143.

Rainer Maria Rilke continues his reflections on the mystery of Mary in this excerpt from his poem "The Life of the Virgin Mary."

THE PRESENTATION OF MARY IN THE TEMPLE

(The Life of the Virgin Mary, 1912)

If you want to comprehend the way she was,
first transpose yourself into a place
teeming with pillars and stairs you can climb,
and archways daring to bridge the abyss
of emptiness remaining inside,
outlining what shapes your identity and
what would be most difficult to remove
without tearing gashes in you.
Once you are there, all is stone and wall,
ascent, vista, and vault—so try
gently pulling the curtain away
in front with both of your hands:
there is a luster of tall and towering things
that take away your breath and elude your touch.
Palace is stacked upon palace, and up
and down run railings, expand, grow wide,
their lines emerging at staggering heights

so your head begins to spin.
Meanwhile, the incense from censers dilutes
proximity; yet what's farthest removed
aims its shimmer directly at you—
and when the light from the votive lamps
plays off your clothes as you slowly approach,
all seeing is hard to endure.

But she came and simply raised her eyes
and at everything she began to look
(a child, a girl among womenfolk).
And then she moved with self-confidence
toward this prideful magnificence,
showing that human buildings are dwarfed
by devotion in one single heart.

She reveled in the pleasure to surrender
to the stirrings awaking in her.
The parents presumed they did dedicate her
and the Almighty had taken her in:
but she who had merely proceeded from them,
was headed past hands unto Providence,
more spacious and massive than house or hall,
and built for her ages ago.

Rainer Maria Rilke, "Presentation of Mary in the Temple,"
in Pictures of God, 28–29.

Reflection Questions

❖ Am I truly aware of, and do I live as, a house or tabernacle wherein the living God dwells?

❖ Do I make sufficient use of the rich tradition of spirituality that comes from the East (Catholic and Orthodox): the lives of the saints, prayers, icons, music?

DECEMBER 8

Solemnity of the Immaculate Conception
of the Blessed Virgin Mary[*]

Readings

Genesis 3:9–15, 20; Ephesians 1:3–6, 11–12; Luke 1:26–38

Historical Note

A feast in honor of Mary's birth appeared in the East in the late sixth century. By the late seventh century, a feast to celebrate the Conception of Mary had developed. A similar feast in honor of the Conception of Mary emerged in the West, in England, in the first half of the eleventh century.

---

[*] This solemnity falls during the Advent season, which prepares us for the coming of Christ at Christmas, and his second coming at the end of time. To prepare for the birth of a child, we look to the mother. Who better understands from experience what the preparation must include? Who better understands the internal movement? Who better grasps the meaning of sacrificial love in the joyful expectation of the moment of birth? It is the mother.

Throughout the Advent season, the Church holds before our contemplative gaze the Mother of Jesus. In a particular way, the readings, prayers, and liturgical texts (both at Mass and in the *Liturgy of the Hours*) reveal how Mary is woven into God's plan for the coming of the Messiah.

However, the liturgical feast of the Immaculate Conception is an excellent illustration of the development of doctrine. Great theologians and saints of the Middle Ages debated the issue of the Immaculate Conception of the Blessed Virgin Mary. All agreed on Mary's preeminent holiness. However, was Mary outside the need for universal salvation? Saints and theologians like Anslem (1033–1109), Bernard (1090–1153), Albert the Great (c.1200–1280), Bonaventure (c. 1217–1274), and Thomas Aquinas (1225–1274) argued that she was not. It was Blessed Duns Scotus (c. 1265–c. 1308) who offered a key insight to develop this doctrine. Duns Scotus argued that Mary was redeemed, preserved free from original sin in anticipation of the redemption Christ won for us. In 1708, Pope Clement XI established the feast as a holy day of obligation. The language of the medieval debate entered the doctrinal formulation of the Church in 1854, in Blessed Pope Pius IX's dogmatic definition of her Immaculate Conception.

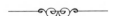

The Catechism of the Catholic Church *states the doctrine of the Immaculate Conception succinctly, incorporating the dogmatic definition of Pius IX. It states:*

Through the centuries the Church has become ever more aware that Mary, "full of grace" through God, was redeemed through the moment of her conception. That is what the

dogma of the Immaculate Conception confesses, as Pope
Pius IX proclaimed in 1854:

> The most Blessed Virgin Mary was, from the first moment
> of her conception, by a singular grace and privilege of
> almighty God and by virtue of the merits of Jesus Christ,
> Savior of the human race, preserved immune from all stain
> of original sin [no. 135 Pius IX, *Ineffabilis Deus*, 1854: DS
> 2803].

From the *Catechism of the Catholic Church*,
(Washington DC: United States Catholic Conference, Inc.
—Libreria Editrice Vaticana, 1994), no. 491.

*On Friday, December 8, 2006, Pope Benedict XVI traveled to Rome's
Piazza di Spagna to pray to the Immaculate Virgin Mary on the occasion of the solemnity. He prayed:*

O Mary, Immaculate Virgin,

Again this year, with filial love, we meet at the foot of
your image to renew to you the homage of the Christian
community and of the city of Rome. Let us pause in prayer
here, following the tradition inaugurated by previous Popes,
on the solemn day in which the liturgy celebrates your
Immaculate Conception, a mystery that is a source of joy and
hope for all the redeemed.

We greet you and call upon you with the Angel's words:
"full of grace" (Lk 1:28), the most beautiful name that God
himself has called you from eternity.

"Full of grace" are you, Mary, full of divine love from the very first moment of your existence, providentially predestined to be Mother of the Redeemer and intimately connected to him in the mystery of salvation. In your Immaculate Conception shines forth the vocation of Christ's disciples, called to become, with his grace, saints and immaculate through love (cf. Eph 1:4). In you shines the dignity of every human being who is always precious in the Creator's eyes. Those who look to you, All Holy Mother, never lose their serenity, no matter what the hardships of life. Although the experience of sin is a sad one since it disfigures the dignity of God's children, anyone who turns to you discovers the beauty of truth and love and finds the path that leads to the Father's house.

"Full of grace," are you, Mary, who, welcoming with your "yes" to the Creator's plan, opened to us the path of salvation. Teach us also at your school to say our "yes" to the Lord's will. Let it be a "yes" that joins with your own "yes," without reservations or shadows, a "yes" that the Heavenly Father willed to have need of in order to beget the new Man, Christ, the one Savior of the world and of history. Give us the courage to say "no" to the deceptions of power, money, pleasure, to dishonest earnings, corruption and hypocrisy, to selfishness and violence; "no" to the Evil One, the deceitful prince of this world; to say "yes" to Christ, who destroys the power of evil with the omnipotence of love. We know that only hearts converted to Love, which is God, can build a better future for all.

"Full of grace," are you, Mary! For all generations your name is a pledge of sure hope. Yes! Because as the great poet Dante wrote, for us mortals you are "a source of living hope"

(*Paradise* XXXIII, 12). Let us come once again as trusting pilgrims to draw faith and comfort, joy and love, safety and peace from this source, the wellspring of your Immaculate Heart.

Virgin "full of grace," show yourself to be a tender and caring Mother to those who live in this city of yours, so that the true Gospel spirit may enliven and guide their conduct; show yourself as Mother and watchful keeper of Italy and Europe, so that people may draw from their ancient Christian roots fresh vigor to build their present and their future; show yourself as a provident and merciful Mother to the whole world so that, by respecting human dignity and rejecting every form of violence and exploitation, sound foundations may be laid for the civilization of love. Show yourself as Mother, especially to those most in need: the defenseless, the marginalized and outcasts, to the victims of a society that all too often sacrifices the human person for other ends and interests.

Show yourself, O Mary, as Mother of all, and give us Christ, the Hope of the world! *"Monstra Te esse Matrem,"* O Virgin Immaculate, full of grace! Amen!

Pope Benedict XVI, "Prayer to Mary Immaculate." *L'Osservatore Romano*. English edition, no. 50, December 13, 2006, p 12.

Georges Bernanos (1888–1948) was born in Paris and died there at the American hospital in Neuilly. His life was like a nomadic existence that brought him from France to Majorca, to Brazil, to France again, to

Tunisia, and back to France. Married, with six children, Bernanos was a soldier in World War I, an essayist, a novelist, and a columnist for Le Figaro, *active in trying to reconcile his Catholic beliefs with political activism. He has been referred to as the "novelist of holiness" (Mauriac) and "the minstrel of grace" (Balthasar). His works articulate the drama of human existence, the struggle to affirm the dignity of the human person, the fight between good and evil, and the ultimate victory of grace over sin.*

In his novel The Diary of a Country Priest *(1936), Bernanos expresses the primacy of grace found in the Immaculate Virgin Mary. In a scene near the end of the novel, an older priest advises the young, dying curé to pray to the Blessed Mother.*

"And what of Our Lady? Do you pray to Our Lady?" "Why, naturally!" "We all say that—but do you pray to her as you should, as befits her? She is our Mother—the mother of all flesh, a new Eve. But she is also our daughter. The ancient world of sorrow, the world before the access of grace, cradled her to its heavy heart for many centuries, dimly awaiting a *virgo genetrix*. For centuries and centuries those ancient hands, so full of sin, cherished the wondrous girl-child whose name even was unknown. A little girl, the queen of the Angels! And she's *still* a little girl, remember! The Middle Ages understood that well enough. They understood everything. But you can't stop fools from reconstructing 'the drama of the Incarnation,' as they call it! ... Think of it! The Word was made flesh and not one of the journalists of those days even knew it was happening! When surely their experience should have taught them that true greatness, even human greatness, genius and courage, love, too—'love' of theirs—it's the devil to recognize 'em! So that ninety-nine

times out of a hundred they have to take bouquets of rheto-
ric to the graves. The dead alone receive their homage. The
blessedness of God! The simplicity of God, that terrible simplicity which damned the pride of the angels. Yes, the devil
must have taken one look at it, and the huge flaming torch at
the peak of creation was plunged down into the night....
That triumphant entry into Jerusalem, for instance—so
lovely! Our Lord deigned to taste of human triumph, as of
other things, as of death. He rejected none of our joys, He
only rejected sin. His death! What a good job of it He made,
not one thing lacking! But His triumph is one for children,
don't you think? There's a painting of Epinal with the baby
donkey and its mother, the palms, and country folk clapping
their hands. A charming, slightly ironical parody of royal
splendour. Our Lord seems to smile. Our Lord often smiles.
He says to us: 'Don't take all these things too seriously,
though there *are* permissible triumphs: as when Joan of Arc
shall ride again into Orleans under flowers and banners, in
fine cloth-of-gold—I don't want her to think she's doing
wrong. As you're so keen on it, My poor babes, I have sanc-
tified your triumph, I have blessed it, as I blessed the wine
from your vineyards.' And it's just the same with miracles.
He performs no more than necessary. Miracles are the pictures—the pretty pictures in the book. But remember this,
lad, Our Lady knew neither triumph nor miracle. Her Son
preserved her from the least tip-touch of the savage wing of
human glory. No one has ever lived, suffered, died in such
simplicity, in such deep ignorance of her own dignity, a dignity crowning her above angels. For she was *born* without
sin—in what amazing isolation! A pool so clear, so pure, that

even her own image—created only for the sacred joy of the Father—was not to be reflected. The Virgin was Innocence. Think what we must seem to her, we humans. Of course, she hates sin, but after all she has never known it, that experience which the holiest saints have never lacked, St. Francis of Assisi himself, seraphic though he may be. The eyes of Our Lady are the only real child-eyes that have ever been raised to our shame and sorrow. Yes, lad, to pray to her as you should, you must feel those eyes of hers upon you: they are not indulgent—for there is no indulgence without something of bitter experience—they are eyes of gentle pity, wondering sadness, and with something more in them, never yet known or expressed, something which makes her younger than sin, younger than the race from which she sprang, and though a mother, by grace, Mother of all grace, our little youngest sister."

Georges Bernanos, *The Diary of a Country Priest*, trans. Pamela Morris (New York: Carroll & Graf Publishers, 1983), 209–12.

Reflection Questions

❖ At the sixth provincial Council of Baltimore, the United States bishops asked the Pope that Mary be named patroness of the United States under the title of the Immaculate Conception. Blessed Pope Pius IX granted their request in 1846. On November 20, 1959, the national shrine of the Immaculate Conception was dedicated in Washington, DC. Have I made a pilgrimage to the shrine?

❖ Does my reflection and prayer on the meaning of this feast bring me to a deeper appreciation for the call to holiness and the beauty of grace in my daily life?

❖ This feast reminds us that Mary's life began at conception. She was Mary from the very first moment of her life. Do I treasure the gift of human life, from the very beginning? Have I confessed any sin of abortion, or encouragement of another to have an abortion, trusting in God's mercy? Do I promote respect for every human life from conception?

DECEMBER 12

*Feast of Our Lady of Guadalupe**

Readings

No readings are assigned to this feast. The readings may come from the lectionary cycle for Ordinary Time, or from the Common of Masses of the Blessed Virgin Mary.

Historical Note

On December 9, 1531, the Virgin Mary appeared to Juan Diego on Tepeyac hill, outside Mexico City. She told him to go to the bishop and tell him her desire that a chapel be built on the spot she would indicate. The Virgin appeared four times to Juan Diego, and a fifth time to his uncle whom she healed his illness. On December 12, she directed Juan Diego to gather flowers from a frozen, barren hilltop and bring them to the bishop of Mexico. When Juan Diego arrived at the bishop's residence, he opened his *tilma* (or cloak), and as the flowers fell to the floor, Juan Diego noticed on the *tilma*

---

*On March 25, 1999, the Congregation for Divine Worship and the Discipline of the Sacraments decreed that this day should be celebrated as a feast in all the countries of the Americas.

the image of the Virgin Mary as she had appeared to him on Tepeyac hill. The image is painted on a cloak of maguey cactus fiber. A pregnant Virgin Mary appears before the sun. Her features are neither Spanish nor Indio, but mestizo. Her foot rests on the crescent moon. Her tunic is covered with flowers and her mantle with stars corresponding to the star chart for the winter of 1531. Convinced that the apparition was authentic, the bishop ordered the construction of the first shrine.

Our Lady of Guadalupe was proclaimed patroness of Mexico in 1737, patroness of the Americas in 1910, and of the Philippines in 1935. When the "Old Basilica" built in 1709 could no longer be used due to earthquakes, the construction of a new one was ordered by the Mexican Episcopal Conference. On October 12, 1976, the image of Our Lady of Guadalupe was installed above the main sanctuary of the new basilica. Pope John Paul II made four apostolic visits to this Mexican shrine (1979, 1990, 1999, 2002). Today the Basilica of Our Lady of Guadalupe is the largest Marian shrine in the world. It is estimated that it draws 20 million pilgrims each year.

Nican Mopohua is the original account written by Antonio Valeriano in Nahuatl, the language spoken by Juan Diego and the Aztecs. Here the words spoken by the Virgin to Juan Diego are paraphrased from the literal translation done by Janet Barber, IHM, of the new Spanish version prepared by the Natuatl scholar, Father Mario Rojas Sanchez.

"Listen, put it into your heart, my youngest and dearest son, that the thing that disturbs you, the thing that afflicts you, is nothing. Do not let your countenance, your heart be disturbed. Do not fear this sickness of your uncle or any other sickness, nor anything that is sharp or hurtful. Am I not here, I who am your Mother? Are you not under my shadow and protection? Am I not the source of your joy? Are you not in the hollow of my mantle, in the crossing of my arms? Do you need anything more? Let nothing else worry you, disturb you. Do not let your uncle's illness worry you, because he will not die now. You may be certain that he is already well."

Franciscan Friars of the Immaculate,
Nican Mopohua, in *A Handbook on Guadalupe*
(New Bedford, MA: Academy of the Immaculate, 1997), 200.

In 1997, a Synod for America was held at the Vatican. From January 22 to 28, 1999, Pope John Paul II traveled to Mexico City and then to St. Louis to mark the closing of a Special Assembly for America of the Synod of Bishops. In Mexico City, he signed the postsynodal apostolic exhortation on the Church in America. On Saturday morning, January 23, approximately five hundred bishops and five thousand priests concelebrated at the papal Mass. Here is an excerpt from the Pope's homily.

I wish to entrust and offer the future of the continent to Blessed Mary, Mother of Christ and of the Church. For this reason, I have the joy now of announcing that I have declared that on December 12 Our Lady of Guadalupe will be celebrated throughout America with the liturgical rank of feast. O Mother! You know the paths followed by the first evangelizers of the New World, from Guanahani Island and Hispaniola to the Amazon forests and the Andean peaks, reaching to Tierra del Fuego in the south and to the Great Lakes and mountains of the north. Accompany the Church which is working in the nations of America, so that she may always preach the Gospel and renew her missionary spirit. Encourage all who devote their lives to the cause of Jesus and the spread of his kingdom. O gentle Lady of Tepeyac, Mother of Guadalupe! To you we present this countless multitude of the faithful praying to God in America. You who have penetrated their hearts, visit and comfort the homes, parishes and dioceses of the whole continent. Grant that Christian families may exemplarily raise their children in the Church's faith and in love of the Gospel, so that they will be the seed of apostolic vocations. Turn your gaze today upon young people and encourage them to walk with Jesus Christ. O Lady and Mother of America! Strengthen the faith of our brothers and sisters, so that in all areas of social, professional, cultural and political life they may act in accord with the truth and the new law which Jesus brought to humanity. Look with mercy on the distress of those suffering from hunger, loneliness, rejection or ignorance. Make us recognize them as your favorite children and give us the fervent charity to help them in their needs. Holy Virgin of Guadalupe, Queen of Peace! Save the nations and peoples of this continent. Teach everyone, political leaders and citizens, to live in true freedom and to act according to the requirements of justice and respect for human rights, so that peace may thus be established once and for all. To you, O Lady of Guadalupe, Mother of Jesus and our Mother, belong all the love, honor, glory and endless praise of your American sons and daughters!

Pope John Paul II. Homily on January 23, 1999, in the Basilica of Our Lady of Guadalupe, Mexico. *L'Osservatore Romano*. English edition, no. 4, January 27, 1999, p. 2.

DECEMBER 20[*]

Mary's Fiat

Readings

On December 20, the Gospel text is taken from St. Luke 1:26–38, the story of the Annunciation.

Father Benedict Groeschel, CFR (1933–), was born on July 23, 1933, in Jersey City, New Jersey, as Peter Groeschel. He entered the Capuchins and took the name Benedict Joseph upon making his profession of vows. He was ordained to the priesthood on June 20, 1959, and later earned a doctorate in psychology.

Father Groeschel served for fourteen years as a chaplain at the Children's Village in Dobbs Ferry, New York. He has taught at Fordham University and several seminaries, and has served as Director for the Office of Spiritual Development for the Archdiocese of New York. He is also the author of nearly three dozen books and many articles. He has produced over one hundred audio and video series on a wide range of religious and spiritual topics.

---

[*]Advent is a time of joyful expectation. From December 17 to December 24, the Church intensifies the time of preparation through its hymns, the "O" Antiphons (prayers used at Evening Prayer that begin with the exclamation "O"), and proper readings assigned to daily Mass.

In 1987, Cardinal O'Connor approved the Franciscan Friars of the Renewal ("Gray Friars"). Father Benedict was a cofounder of the community, and has served as its superior and almoner (one who obtains and distributes alms to the poor).

Here Father Groeschel reflects on Mary's words at the Annunciation.

These are the most important words ever spoken by a mortal human being. Only the words of Christ himself can be more important than these words, which are often called Mary's *fiat*, that is, "let it be done." On behalf of the whole human race, Mary says yes to God.

How much there is for us to learn from her consent. Fourteen hundred years later inquisitors would ask Joan of Arc, "Why would God choose a little peasant girl?" Her response is powerful in its simplicity and reminds us somewhat of the mystery of the Annunciation to Mary. "I suppose He wanted to choose a little peasant girl," Joan said. Bernadette Soubirous would answer the same question in the same way centuries later. It is not wise for mortal men to attempt to read God's mind, but we can say at least that He wanted to show that His grace and salvation did not depend on what humans deserve. The angel's greeting, "Highly favored one" or "full of grace," shows that God had very clearly prepared His handmaid for her task. This was no accident or random event of nature. He comes, He opens, and no one shuts. And yet, how moving and fitting it is that Mary must consent. The world was lost by a young woman's decision, and it was saved in the same way. At least since the second century Eve and Mary have been seen as mysteriously related. The early Christian writers called Mary the new Eve and her Son the new Adam. Our meditations now move us into the most profound spiritual mysteries. The focus turns from what we do to respond to God to a contemplation of what He has done for us. O Key of David and Scepter of the house of Israel: You open and no one closes; You close and no one opens. Come, and deliver from the chains of prison those who sit in darkness and in the shadow of death.

PRAYER

Lord God, open my being to the wonder of Your grace and let me never again take lightly the mystery of salvation. Open, and let no one close my heart to the mystery of Your Emmanuel and His Mother, whom You chose and who in awe and obedience responded by saying yes to Your messenger. Amen.

Benedict Groeschel, CFR, *Behold, He Comes: Meditations on the Incarnation* (Ann Arbor, MI: Servant Publications/St. Anthony Messenger Press, 2001), 57–58.

Reflection Questions

❖ The liturgical cycle of the Church year, that is, Advent, Lent, and so forth, highlights different moments in the history of salvation. Does the Advent season help me to grow in appreciation for Mary's unique role in the mystery of the Incarnation?

❖ As Christmas approaches, do I reflect on the role of the Virgin Mary as she is found in the popular carols and in art?

The Christmas Season

St. Louis Marie de Montfort (1673–1716) was the founder of two religious congregations: the Sisters of Divine Wisdom (1703) and the Missionaries of the Company of Mary (1715). He wrote many works on the Blessed Mother. In his work True Devotion to the Blessed Virgin, *he reflects on Mary's role in the mystery of the Incarnation.*

16. God the Father gave his only Son to the world only through Mary.... The Son of God became man only in Mary and through Mary. God the Holy Spirit formed Jesus Christ in Mary but only after having asked her consent through one of the chief ministers of his court.

St. Louis Marie de Montfort, *True Devotion to the Blessed Virgin*
(Bay Shore, NY: Montfort Publications, 1980), 6–7.

Gertrude von le Fort (1876–1971) was a prolific author and poet who was born in Westphalia, Germany. Following the death of her father, she made a trip to Rome, Italy, that had a significant impact on her life. She studied theology, history, and philosophy at several German universi-

ties. In 1926, she converted to Catholicism. She traveled and lectured extensively throughout Italy, Switzerland, and Germany. In her writing, she explored religious questions within a historic context. Her novel The Song at the Scaffold, *based on the experience of the martyrdom of a French Carmelite community of nuns during the French Revolution, became the basis for the opera* The Dialogues of the Carmelites.

CHRISTMAS

Your voice speaks:
Little child out of Eternity, now will I sing to
Thy Mother!
The song shall be fair as dawn-tinted snow.
Rejoice Mary Virgin, daughter of my earth,
sister of my soul,
rejoice, O joy of my joy!
I am as one who wanders through the night,
but you are a house
under stars.
I am a thirsty cup, but you are God's open sea.
Rejoice Mary Virgin, blessed are those who
call you blessed,
never more shall child of man lose hope.
I am one love for all, I shall never cease from
saying: one of you
has been exalted by the Lord.
Rejoice Mary Virgin, wings of my earth, crown
of my soul, rejoice
joy of my joy!
Blessed are those who call you blessed.

Gertrude von le Fort, "Christmas," in *I Sing of a Maiden*, trans. Margaret Chanler Therese (New York: Macmillan, 1947), http://campus.udayton.edu/mary/resources/poetry/xmasp4.html.

Mary Catherine Brennan meditates on the thoughts that might have filled Mary's heart on that first Christmas night, and casts a glance into what the future will bring.

LET US GO OVER TO BETHLEHEM

What thoughts, O tender Mother, filled
Your heart that Christmas night?
Of that high moment when you heard
From God's own acolyte.

"The Lord is with thee. Blessed, thou ..."
That you might souls unbind
That all of heaven looked to you
And all of humankind;

Did you relive exultant joys,
And days of journeying
That led to your aged cousin's home
Through valley's bright with Spring,

Or gazing on your new-born Son

See Cana; Calvary—
Beyond the lantern's dimming rays
A million altars see

Whose light would spell eternal Love,

With solace, strength for men;
And songs that echoed Bethlehem
Bring holy peace

If we draw near the hallowed cave

As shepherds did that morn,
You'll whisper all that filled your heart
That night our Christ was born.

Mary Catherine Brennan, "Let Us Go Over to Bethlehem,"
in *Mary Immaculate: God's Mother and Mine*
(New York: Marist Press, 1946), "Christmas Poems"
http://campus.udayton.edu/mary/resources/poetry/xmasp3.html.

Virginia Kimball (1940–) is the mother of nine children. She earned a doctorate in sacred theology from the International Marian Research Institute at the University of Dayton. She has taught at the University of Dayton and currently serves as an adjunct faculty member at Assumption College in Worcester, Massachusetts. She has served as President of the Mariological Society of America, and as Vice President of the Ecumenical Society of the Blessed Virgin Mary of the U.S.A. In her poem "A Moment of Nativity," she reflects on the tender quality of Mary's maternal love on that first Christmas Day.

A MOMENT OF NATIVITY

It is a tender, grasping little fist
that wraps her finger mightily that day,
so small and warm, holding tightly on ...

timely bond of mother with newborn life.
This mother's love is ageless, a sweet kiss
on a son's cuddled, moist head her way ...
discovering a gift of love upon
the red birthing mat in cold darkened cave.

He's a gift of light from God, of touching,
a truth divinely lent as she nurses,
creation's miracle always spinning
in fresh moments of eternal birthing.
So fondly in a brief glimpse of clutching,
the infinite bubbles out. In curses
of darkness, amid separation—winds
of loneliness from God—Life bathing

in the midwife's washing pool
thrusts fragile child, like a fool

into still frigid water of our days
soon surely swirling with the Spirit's warmth.
Can we remember what the prophet says?
We forget. Forget! As the mother's breast
spills calming milk into his rooting mouth,
we hope for God's strength in the coming test.

She smiles and timeless tiny one gurgles:
through that door of hope, a door ajar ...
Life forms creation's gentle realm of flesh,
enlightening the mother's waiting heart,
insight to GLORY in the Christmas crèche....

Virginia Kimball, "A Moment of Nativity" in "Christmas Poems,"
http://campus.udayton.edu/mary/resources/poetry/xmasp6.html.

St. Augustine was an enormously popular preacher. Both Catholics and non-Catholics flocked to hear him preach both in his own Diocese of Hippo, and to other dioceses where he had been invited to speak. Stenographers copied down and transcribed his sermons. As his popularity grew, collections of his sermons were made and found their way to Europe. In this sermon, St. Augustine reflects on the joy of Christmas, the day in which we celebrate the birth of Christ who was born of the Virgin Mary.

1. . . . The virgin mother indeed provided a demonstration of his greatness, being found a virgin after giving birth just as she was a virgin before conceiving, being found, not put, with child by her husband; without male intervention carrying a male in her womb; all the more blessed and admirable for receiving the gift of fertility without losing that of integrity. They prefer to regard this stupendous miracle as fiction rather than fact. Thus in Christ, true God and true man, they despise the human because they cannot believe it; they do not believe the divine because they cannot despise it. We, however, find the body of man in the humility of God all the more welcome, the more contemptible it seems to them; and the more they think it is impossible, the more divine it seems to us that a man was born by a virgin bringing forth.

2. So then, let us celebrate the birthday of the Lord with all due festive gatherings. Let men rejoice, let women rejoice. Christ has been born, a man; he has been born of a woman; and each sex has been honored. Now therefore, let everyone,

having been condemned in the first man, pass over to the second. It was a woman who sold us death; a woman who bore us life. *The likeness of the flesh of sin* (Rom. 8:3) has been born, so that the flesh of sin may be cleansed and purified. And thus it is not the flesh that is to be faulted, but the fault that must die in order that the nature may live; because one has been born without fault, in whom the other who was at fault may be reborn.... *Rejoice, you just* (Ps 33:1); it is the birthday of the Justifier. Rejoice, you who are weak and sick; it is the birthday of the Savior, the Healer. Rejoice, captives; it is the birthday of the Redeemer. Rejoice, slaves; it is the birthday of the one who makes you lords. Rejoice, free people; it is the birthday of the one who makes you free. Rejoice, all Christians; it is the birthday of Christ.

3. Born of his mother, he commended this day to the ages, while born of his Father he created all ages. That birth could have no mother, while this one required no man as father. To sum up, Christ was born both of a Father and of a mother; both without a father and without a mother; of a Father as God, of a mother as man; without a mother as God, without a father as man. Therefore, *who will recount his begetting* (Is 53:8), whether that one without time or this one without seed; that one without beginning or this one without precedent; that one which never was not, or this one which never was before or after; that one which has no end, or this one which has its beginning in its end? Rightly therefore did the prophets foretell that he would be born, while the heavens and the angels announced that he had been. The one who holds the world in being was lying in a manger; he was simultaneously speechless infant and Word. The heavens

cannot contain him, a woman carried him in her bosom. She was ruling our ruler, carrying the one in whom we are, suckling our bread. O manifest infirmity and wondrous humility in which was thus concealed total divinity! Omnipotence was ruling the mother on whom infancy was depending; was nourishing on truth the mother whose breasts it was sucking. May he bring his gifts to perfection in us, since he did not shrink from making his own our tiny beginnings; and may he make us into children of God, since for our sake he was willing to be made a child of man.

St. Augustine, "Sermon 184—On Christmas Day," in *Sermons* III/6 (184–229Z), trans. Edmund Hill, OP. *The Works of St. Augustine: A Translation for the 21st Century*, ed. John E. Rotelle, OSA (New Rochelle, NY: New City Press, 1993), 17, 18, 19.

Hail Mary, full of grace,
the Lord is with thee!
Blessed art thou among women
and blessed is the fruit of your womb, Jesus.
Holy Mary, Mother of God,
pray for us sinners,
now and at the hour of our death.
Amen.

Acknowledgments

We acknowledge and thank those publishers whose material, whether in the public domain or under copyright protection, has made this work possible. Every effort has been made to obtain all the proper permissions. But if we have inadvertently not obtained a required permission, we ask the publisher to contact the editor for proper acknowledgement and compensation.

We wish to express a special word of thanks for the use of the material listed in this book:

Unless otherwise noted, all excerpts from Pope Paul VI, Pope John Paul II, and Pope Benedict XVI are copyright © Libreria Editrice Vaticana and are used with permission.

Alighieri, Dante. Canto XXXIII: 1–42 of "The Paradiso." From *The Divine Comedy* by Dante Alighieri, translated by John Ciardi. Copyright 1954, 1957, 1960, 1961, 1965, 1967, 1970 by the Ciardi Family Publishing Trust. Used by permission of W. W. Norton & Company, Inc.

Andrew of Crete. *The Liturgy of the Hours* IV. New York: Catholic Book Publishing Co., 1975. © 1974 International Committee on English in the Liturgy, Inc. All rights reserved. Used with permission.

Augustine. "Holy Virginity." From *The Works of St. Augustine*. Edited by John E. Torelle, OSA. Translated by Ray Kearney. Vol. 9. Hyde Park, NY: New City Press, 1999. Used with permission from the Augustinian Heritage Institute.

———. "Sermon 184– On Christmas Day." From *Sermons* III/6 (184–229Z). Translated by Edmund Hill, OP. *The Works of St. Augustine: A Translation for the 21st Century*. Edited by John E. Rotelle, OSA. New Rochelle, NY: New City Press, 1993. Used with permission from the Augustinian Heritage Institute.

Bello, Antonio. *Mary: Human and Holy*. Translated by Paul Duggan. Boston: Pauline Books & Media, 2000. Used with permission.

Benedict XVI. "Prayer to Mary Immaculate." *L'Osservatore Romano*. English ed. no. 50. December 13, 2006.

Bernanos, George. *The Diary of a Country Priest*. Reprinted with the permission of Scribner, an imprint of Simon & Schuster Adult Publishing Group, from *The Diary of a Country Priest*, translated by Pamela Morris. Copyright © 1937 by The Macmillan Company. Copyright renewed © 1965 by Macmillan Company. All rights reserved.

Bernard of Clairvaux. "Sermon for the Feast of the Nativity of the Blessed Virgin Mary." From *St. Bernard's Sermons for the Seasons and Principal Festivals of the Year*. Translated by a priest of Mount Melleray. Vol. 3. Westminster, ME: Carroll Press, 1950.

Book of Akathists. New York: Holy Trinity Monastery, 1994. Used with permission.

Brennan, Mary Catherine. "Let Us Go Over to Bethlehem." From *Mary Immaculate: God's Mother and Mine*. New York: Marist Press, 1946. http://campus.udayton.edu/mary/resources/poetry/xmasp3.html.

Carretto, Carlo. *Blessed Are You Who Believed*. Translated by Barbara Well. Maryknoll, NY: Orbis, 1982. Used with permission.

Catechism of the Catholic Church. No. 491. © Libreria Editrice Vaticana/ United States Conference of Catholic Bishops, 2001. Used with permission.

Congregation for the Sacraments and Divine Worship. "Introduction." From "Order of Crowning an Image of the Blessed Virgin Mary." From *The Rites of the Catholic Church* as Revised by the Second Vatican Ecumenical Council. Vol. 2. Study ed. Collegeville, MN: Pueblo Book/Liturgical Press, 1991. Used with permission.

de Liguori, Alphonsus Maria. *The Glories of Mary*. 2nd ed. London: Burns, Oates & Washbourne, 1868.

de Montfort, Louis Marie. *True Devotion to the Blessed Virgin*. Bay Shore, NY: Montfort Publications, 1980. Used with permission.

Doherty, Catherine de Hueck. *Bogoroditza: She Who Gave Birth to God*. Compiled by Linda Lambeth. Combermere, Ontario: Madonna

House Publications, 1998. Used with permission. www.madonna house .org/publications.

Ephrem. *Nicene and Post-Nicene Fathers of the Christian Church*. 2nd series. Vol. 13. Grand Rapids, MI: Eerdmans, 1983. Used with permission.

Eymard, Peter Julian. *Our Lady of the Blessed Sacrament*. Cleveland, OH: Emmanuel Publications, 1930. Used with permission.

Franciscan Friars of the Immaculate. *Nican Mopohua*. From *A Handbook on Guadalupe*. New Bedford, MA: Academy of the Immaculate, 1997. Used with permission.

Giaquinta, William. "The Life of Mary: A Prayer." Used with permission from the Pro Sanctity Movement.

Gingras, George E., PhD, ed., anno. Excerpts from *Egeria: Diary of a Pilgrimage* © 1997, Rev. Johannes Quasten, Rev. Walter J. Burghardt, SJ, and Thomas Comerford Lawler. Paulist Press, Inc., New York/Mahwah, NJ. Reprinted by permission of Paulist Press, Inc. www.paulistpress.com.

Groeschel, Benedict, CFR. *Behold, He Comes: Meditations on the Incarnation*. Ann Arbor, MI: Servant, 2001. Published by Servant Books, used with permission of St. Anthony Messenger Press. www.american catholic.org.

Guardini, Romano. *The Rosary of Our Lady*. Translated by H. von Schuecking. Manchester, NH: Sophia Institute Press, 1994. Used with permission.

Hahn, Scott. *Hail Holy Queen: The Mother of God in the Word of God*. New York: Doubleday, 2001. Used with permission.

Hickey, James. *Mary at the Foot of the Cross*. San Francisco: Ignatius Press, 1988. Reprinted with permission of Ignatius Press, San Francisco.

Hopko, Thomas. *The Orthodox Faith: An Elementary Handbook on the Orthodox Church*. Vol. 2. *Worship*. New York: Department of Religious Education of the Orthodox Church in America, 1976. Used with permission of The Orthodox Church in America. www.oca.org.

Houselander, Caryll. *The Reed of God*. Excerpted from *The Reed of God*, © 2006. Used with permission from the publisher, Christian Classics, Notre Dame, Indiana. www.avemariapress.com.

Iranaeus. *Against the Heresies* V, XIX, 1–2. From *The Anti-Nicene Fathers.* Edited by Reverend Alexander Roberts, DD, and James Donaldson, LLD. Vol. 1. New York: Charles Scribner's Sons, 1903.

John XXIII. *Holy Rosary.* From *Journal of a Soul.* Translated by Dorothy White. New York: Signet, 1965. Used with permission.

John of Damascus. *On the Orthodox Faith* III. In *Nicene and Post-Nicene Fathers of the Christian Church.* 2nd series. Edited by Philip Schaff, DD, LLD, and Henry Wace, DD. Vol. 9. Grand Rapids, MI: Eerdmans, 1983.

John of the Cross. "Del Verbo Divino." From *The Collected Works of St. John of the Cross.* Translated by Kieran Kavanaugh and Otilio Rodriguez. Copyright © 1964, 1979, 1991 by Washington Province of Discalced Carmelites. ICS Publications. 2131 Lincoln Road, NE. Washington, DC 20002-1199 USA. www.icspublcations.org.

John Paul II. *Ecclesia de Eucharistia.* Boston: Pauline Books & Media, 2003. Used with permission.

———. Homily at Mass in Fatima. *L'Osservatore Romano.* English edition. May 17, 1982. Used with permission.

———. Homily at the Basilica of Our Lady of Guadalupe, Mexico, on January 23, 1999. *L'Osservatore Romano.* English ed. no. 4. January 27, 1999. Used with permission.

———. Prayer at Lourdes. *L'Osservatore Romano.* English edition, no. 34. August 25, 2004. Used with permission.

———. *Redemptor Hominis.* Washington, DC: United States Catholic Conference, 1979.

———. *Redemptoris Mater.* Boston: Pauline Books & Media, 1987. Used with permission.

———. *Theotokos. Woman, Mother, Disciple: A Catechesis on Mary, Mother of God.* Boston: Pauline Books & Media, 2000. Used with permission.

Kimball, Virginia. "A Moment of Nativity." From "Christmas Poems." http://campus.udayton.edu/mary/resources/poetry/xmasp6.html. Revised version used with permission of author.

Marmion, Dom Columba. *Christ in His Mysteries.* St. Louis, MO: Herder Books, 1939.

Newman, John Henry. *Prayers, Verses and Devotions*. San Francisco, Ignatius Press, 2000. Reprinted with permission of Ignatius Press, San Francisco.

Nolan, Mary Catherine, O.P. *Mary's Song*. Excerpted from *Mary's Song*, © 2001. Used with permission from the publisher, Ave Maria Press, Notre Dame, Indiana. www.avemariapress.com.

O'Donnell, Christopher, O.Carm. *At Worship with Mary: A Pastoral and Theological Study*. Illustrated by Placid Stuckenschneider, OSB. Wilmington, DE: Michael Glazier, 1988. Used with permission.

Paul VI. *Marialis Cultus*. Boston: Daughters of St. Paul, 1974. Used with permission.

———. "Nazareth a Model." From *The Liturgy of the Hours*. Vol. I. New York: Catholic Book Publishing Co., 1975. © 1974, International Committee on English in the Liturgy, Inc. All rights reserved. Used with permission.

Pius XII. *Ad Caeli Reginam* (October 11, 1954). From *The Papal Encyclicals 1939–1958*. Claudia Carlen, IHM. Raleigh, NC: McGrath Publishing, 1981. Used with permission.

———. *Munificentissimus Deus*. From *The Christian Faith*. Edited by Jacques Dupuis. 7th rev. ed. New York: Alba House, 2001. Used with permission.

Powers, Jessica. "The Cloud of Carmel." From *The Selected Poetry of Jessica Powers*. Edited by Regina Siegfried, ASC, and Robert Morneau. Washington, DC: ICS Publications, 1999. All copyrights Carmelite Monastery, Pewaukee, Wisconsin. Used with permission.

Rahner, Hugo, SJ. *Our Lady and the Church*. From *Our Lady and the Church*, translated by Rev. Sebastian Bullough, © 1961 by Darton, Longman & Todd, Ltd. Used by permission of Pantheon Books, a division of Random House, Inc.

Ratzinger, Joseph. "The Message of the Basilica of Saint Mary Major in Rome." From *Images of Hope: Meditations on Major Feasts*. Translated by John Rock and Graham Harrison. San Francisco: Ignatius Press, 2006. Reprinted with permission of Ignatius Press, San Francisco.

Regina Caeli. From the *Manual of Indulgences*. Translation into English from the 4th ed. (2006) of *Enchiridion Indulgentiarum Normae et*

Concessiones (1999). Washington, DC: United States Conference of Catholic Bishops, 2006. English translation copyright © 2006, Libreria Editrice Vaticana.

Rilke, Rainer Maria. "The Birth of Mary" and "The Presentation of Mary in the Temple." From *Pictures of God: Rilke's Religious Poetry, Including "The Life of the Virgin Mary."* Translated by Annemarie S. Kidder. Livonia, MI: First Page Publications, 2005. Used with permission.

Rupp, Joyce. *Your Sorrow Is My Sorrow.* New York: Crossroads Publishing Company, 1999. Reproduced with permission of the Crossroad Publishing Company via Copyright Clearance Center.

Sheen, Fulton J. *Life of Christ.* New York: Doubleday/Image, 1977. Used with permission.

———. *Seven Words of Jesus and Mary: Lessons from Cana and Calvary.* Used by permission from Seven Words of Jesus and Mary: Lessons on Cana and Calvary, (c) 2001, Liguori Publications, Ligouri, MO 63057, USA. www.liguori.org.

Vann, Gerald, OP. *The Seven Swords.* London: Sheed & Ward, 1953.

Vereb, Jerome M., CP. *Pope John Paul II and the Luminous Mysteries of the Rosary.* Excerpts from *Pope John Paul II and the Luminous Mysteries of the Rosary* are reproduced with permission, © 2003 by Catholic Book Publishing Corp., NJ. All rights reserved. www.catholicbookpublishing.com.

von Balthasar, Hans Urs. *Theo-Drama.* Translated by Graham Harrison. Vol. 4. San Francisco: Ignatius Press, 1994. Reprinted with permission of Ignatius Press, San Francisco.

von le Fort, Gertrude. "Christmas." From *I Sing of Maiden: The Mary Book of Verse.* New York: Macmillan, 1947.

von Speyr, Adrienne. *Handmaid of the Lord.* Translated by E.A. Nelson. San Francisco: Ignatius Press, 1985. Reprinted with permission of Ignatius Press, San Franscisco.

Ward, Masie. *The Splendor of the Rosary.* New York: Sheed & Ward, 1945.

Select Bibliography

Buono, Anthony M. *The Greatest Marian Prayers*. New York: Alba House, 1999.

Crichton, J. D. *Our Lady in the Liturgy*. Blackrock, Dublin: Columba Press, 1997.

Dictionary of Mary. New York: Catholic Book Publishing Co., 1985.

Dupuis, Jacques, ed. *The Christian Faith: In the Doctrinal Documents of the Catholic Church*. 7th ed. New York: Alba House, 2001.

Nuovo Dizionario di Mariologia. Milano: Edizioni Paoline. 1985.

O'Carroll, Michael, CSSp. *Theotokos: A Theological Encyclopedia of the Blessed Virgin Mary*. Wilmington, DE: Michael Glazier, 1982.

O'Donnell, Christopher, O.Carm. "Core Marian Themes in the Carmelite Order: Patroness, Mother, Sister, Most Pure Virgin." In *Carmel and Mary*. Edited by John F. Welch, OCarm. Washington, DC: Carmelite Institute, 2002.

Smet, Joachim. O.Carm. *The Carmelites: A History of the Brothers of Our Lady of Mount Carmel*. Vol. 1. Darien, IL: Carmelite Spiritual Center, 1988.

ROSEMARY VACCARI MYSEL is a former managing editor at Simon & Schuster who works now as a freelance editor. She has taught sacramental preparation in parish religious education programs in New Jersey and in Florida, where she lives with her husband and four children.

MSGR. ANDREW VACCARI is the Chancellor of the Diocese of Brooklyn, New York, and a member of the Canon Law Society of America, who offers various courses in Adult Religious Education. A popular retreat leader, Monsignor has also led pilgrimages to Italy, the Holy Land, and Spain with his brother, Father Peter Vaccari.

REV. PETER VACCARI is a member of the faculty of the Seminary of the Immaculate Conception in Huntington, New York, where he teaches Church history and serves as a spiritual director. He is a member of the American Catholic Historical Association, who has also preached retreats and lectured in Adult Religious Education programs. He is co-author of the popular history *Diocese of Immigrants: The Brooklyn Catholic Experience, 1853–2003* (Strasbourg, France: Editions du Signe, 2004).

auline
BOOKS & MEDIA

The Daughters of St. Paul operate book and media centers at the following addresses. Visit, call or write the one nearest you today, or find us on the World Wide Web, www.pauline.org.

CALIFORNIA
3908 Sepulveda Blvd, Culver City, CA 90230	310-397-8676
2640 Broadway Street, Redwood City, CA 94063	650-369-4230
5945 Balboa Avenue, San Diego, CA 92111	858-565-9181

FLORIDA
145 S.W. 107th Avenue, Miami, FL 33174	305-559-6715

HAWAII
1143 Bishop Street, Honolulu, HI 96813	808-521-2731
Neighbor Islands call:	866-521-2731

ILLINOIS
172 North Michigan Avenue, Chicago, IL 60601	312-346-4228

LOUISIANA
4403 Veterans Memorial Blvd, Metairie, LA 70006	504-887-7631

MASSACHUSETTS
885 Providence Hwy, Dedham, MA 02026	781-326-5385

MISSOURI
9804 Watson Road, St. Louis, MO 63126	314-965-3512

NEW JERSEY
561 U.S. Route 1, Wick Plaza, Edison, NJ 08817	732-572-1200

NEW YORK
150 East 52nd Street, New York, NY 10022	212-754-1110

PENNSYLVANIA
9171-A Roosevelt Blvd, Philadelphia, PA 19114	215-676-9494

SOUTH CAROLINA
243 King Street, Charleston, SC 29401	843-577-0175

TENNESSEE
4811 Poplar Avenue, Memphis, TN 38117	901-761-2987

TEXAS
114 Main Plaza, San Antonio, TX 78205	210-224-8101

VIRGINIA
1025 King Street, Alexandria, VA 22314	703-549-3806

CANADA
3022 Dufferin Street, Toronto, ON M6B 3T5	416-781-9131

¡También somos su fuente para libros,
videos y música en español!